T0168236

Humor and Comedy in Puppetry

Humor and Comedy in Puppetry: Celebration in Popular Culture

Edited by
Dina Sherzer and Joel Sherzer

Bowling Green State University Popular Press
Bowling Green, Ohio 43403

Library of Congress Catalogue Card No.:   87-72220

ISBN: 0-87972-412-9 Clothbound
      0-87972-413-7 Paperback

Contents

Introduction   1
  Dina Sherzer and Joel Sherzer
Humor and Puppets   8
  Antonio Pasqualino
The Cocreation of the Comic in Puppetry   30
  Frank Proschan
Verbal Humor in the Puppet Theater   47
  Dina Sherzer and Joel Sherzer
The Clown Figure in the Puppet Theater of West Java:
  The Ancestor and the Individual   65
  Kathy Foley
Functions of the Comic Attendants
  (*Panasar*) in a Balinese Shadowplay   79
  Fredrik E. deBoer
The Form and Function of Humor in the Liège
  Puppet Theater   106
  Joan Gross
Humor and Anti-Humor in Western Puebloan
  Puppetry Performances   127
  M. Jane Young
Contributors   151

Introduction

Dina and Joel Sherzer

This volume is about puppetry, an expression of popular and folk culture which is extremely widespread around the world and yet has attracted relatively little scholarly attention. Puppetry, which is intended for audiences of adults as well as children, is a form of communication and entertainment and an esthetic and artistic creation. Of the many aspects of puppetry worthy of scholarly study, our focus is on a central and dominant feature—humor and comedy.

The papers collected here deal with traditional puppetry. It is possible and sometimes useful to make a distinction between traditional and modern or contemporary puppetry. Traditional puppetry is part of ongoing folk culture and is felt by members of the communities in which it is found to be historically old, a continuation of the past. Modern or contemporary puppetry on the other hand involves newly invented, individual forms. At the same time, it is important to recognize that the break between traditional and modern puppetry is not always a sharp one. As all of the papers in this volume indicate, traditional puppetry is continually innovating, adapting itself to new situations in a constantly changing world. And all new forms of puppetry, even if invented yesterday, draw on many features and techniques that have always been characteristic of puppets.

Puppets are performing objects,[1] gloves, rods, animal skins, scrolls, masks, and in interesting cases, even humans, such as *wayang wong* in Indonesia. The inanimate objects become animate through the, usually hidden, activities of the puppeteer, who makes these objects perform— walk, talk, sing, dance, burp, fart, and laugh. It is this disparity and intersection between the animate and the inanimate, the human and the non-human which is at the heart of the humor of puppets. Ironically, because they are not human, puppets can do more and get away with more than humans.

Puppetry integrates many semiotic streams, codes, and channels, interacting and intersecting in fascinating and complicated ways. These include colors, costumes, gestures and body movements, dance, music,

1

physical traits, and staging, as well as language. Puppets are both a reflection of and a metacommunicative commentary on the society and culture in which they are performed. Therefore conventional iconography and symbolism are important features. In sum, puppets are an extremely vibrant, rich, and complex form of popular culture, involving both social and individual creativity and expression. In addition, they constitute an escape from, commentary on, and source of inspiration for high and elite forms of cultural expression.

As is discussed by Frank Proschan, puppet shows are not fixed and frozen in form. Rather they are a cocreation of puppeteer and audience. In this sense, puppet shows are dialogic (actually polylogic, since they are the product of an interaction among puppeteer, puppets, and audience) rather than monologic, and performances thus have an emergent quality to them. What happens on a puppet stage is the result of codes and rules, expectations and assumptions with regard to performance and interpretation, that are rooted in performance traditions and are shared by puppeteers and audiences. These codes, rules, expectations, and assumptions have been transmitted for generations, mostly orally, but in writing as well. An example is the complicated set of gestures and physical traits of Italian puppets, which are described in detail by Antonio Pasqualino. In addition, puppetry is a very self-reflexive expression; through puppetry people look at themselves, their social and cultural life, their history and traditions, and their rituals.

In addition to being an intersection of puppeteer and audience, puppet shows also involve an intersection of texts and textual sources of various kinds. This intertextuality, the revitalization, recreation, transcreation, mingling, and mixing of texts, is a feature of all of the puppet traditions studied in this volume. Intertextuality takes various forms. The Sicilian and Belgian traditions, studied by Antonio Pasqualino and Joan Gross, enact the well-known medieval epic of the *Song of Roland*, the story of the knights of Charlemagne and their fight against the Saracens. Indonesian puppetry, studied by Frederik E. deBoer and Kathy Foley, enacts Indian myths, the *Mahabharata* and the *Ramayana*. Similarly, as studied here by Jane Young, Western Puebloan Indian puppets enact traditional myths.

The study of puppetry is of relevance to a variety of scholarly disciplines and orientations, including anthropology, folklore, linguistics, literature, and semiotics, as well as to the general study of popular culture. Anthropology has tended to treat puppetry, like other forms of popular folk esthetic expression, as marginal to its central concerns, except in places like Bali, and Java, where it is obviously intimately linked to religion and ritual. And yet puppetry is most relevant to anthropology, as a rich expression of native esthetics, visual and verbal, as a reflection of and commentary on social and political structure, and as a major form of leisure entertainment. Puppetry is a fascinating manifestation of material, visual, and verbal folklore, integrating music, dance, language, and art. For linguistics, especially sociolinguistics, puppet theaters provide the gamut of social and dialectal forms in use in a community. In addition, by manipulating and playing with language in all sorts of ways, puppets reveal aspects of linguistic structure and especially creative potential not expressed in ordinary and normative language use. Puppetry presents literary classics as old as the *Mahabharata* and the *Song of Roland*, but at the same time offers playful, innovative and satirical versions of them, together with new and creatively innovative literary forms.

Puppetry is a celebration of the dynamism and diversity of popular culture. In traditional, folk, and popular puppetry we find many processes and techniques which are basic to such twentieth century artistic movements as Dadaism, Russian Futurism, and the Theater of the Absurd and these avant-garde movements have indeed been influenced by puppetry.

Puppet scholarship tends to concern itself with historical matters—the origins, developments, and geographic spread of puppet traditions; the physical characteristics of puppets—how they are constructed; or the stories they tell.[2] In some of the places in the world, such as Indonesia, where puppetry is a major and central feature of the culture, and constitutes high as well popular culture, its relationship to such areas as religion and ritual is discussed in the literature.[3] Puppetry is so important in the social, cultural, and artistic life of such Indonesian islands as Bali and Java that schools for *dalangs* (puppeteers) are found there. In eastern Europe, especially Czechoslovakia, where folk puppetry is a vital aspect of traditional culture, and which has been a center of the development of semiotics, there exists an interesting body of literature dealing with semiotic approaches to puppetry.[4]

In recent years, there has been increasing recognition of the significance of puppetry. This recognition has led to important publications, written from the integrated perspectives of folklore, anthropology, linguistics, literary criticism, and semiotics.[5] Play, humor, and comedy, however, although so essential to and so characteristic of puppetry, have not been the focus of sustained theoretical and empirical discussion. Thus the significance of this volume.

Puppetry offers a particularly valuable contribution to the study of play, humor, and comedy. For whatever else puppets are and do, they are funny. The sources of and the forms of puppet play and humor are explored in all of the papers in this volume. These include the nature of puppets themselves—inanimate, often small objects behaving like humans and animals; physical buffoonery and slapstick; an exuberance of word play; stereotyping, gross exaggeration, and degradation of human and animal behaviors; ethnic and social caricature; exaggeration and play with well-known stories or story types; humor of situation and circumstance; the incorporation of comical, clown-like figures; social, political, and individual satire and commentary; breaking of ordinary rules of social etiquette; scatological and sexual behavior not permitted by performing humans; metacommunicative commentary; and interaction with and especially tricking of members of the audience.

As the papers in this volume demonstrate, there are many similarities across cultures and traditions in the types of comedy and humor that are expressed in puppets, including slapstick, buffoonery, word play, satire and caricature, and the breaking of social rules. Some of these similarities are due to diffusion across space and time. Thus Punch, Polichinelle, Pulcinella, Petrushka, Aragoz, and Karagoz are all historically related traditions. Other similarities are due to the nature of puppets themselves. Over and over around the world, these inanimate, usually small objects seem appropriate for outrageously poking fun at others, oneself, and one's society and its mechanical and arbitrary conventions and norms and for debasing high culture.

Central to puppet play and comedy is a web of intersecting incongruities—big/small, animate/inanimate, human/object, talking/non-talking or talked for, adult/child, having volume/flat, high culture/folk or popular culture, serious/humorous, and contrasting languages, registers, styles, dialects, and non-verbal gestures. As Antonio Pasqualino points out, these incongruities themselves become a source of further, humorous incongruities, as when a strong and powerful character trembles or stutters with fear.

Puppet play, humor, and comedy are significant for a number of reasons. Puppets celebrate the diversity of popular culture, linguistically, socially, and individually, in contrast to official, elite, and standardizing high culture, to which puppets are a comic counterpoint and which they often debase. Puppets constantly and dangerously test the boundaries of the licit and the illicit, the permitted and the unpermitted. Puppets are a parody, of customs, of proper social behavior and rules of etiquette and politeness, of the very textual sources that they are based on, and even sometimes, of themselves. Frederik E. deBoer's paper on the comic attendants in Balinese shadowplays provides examples of such manipulations.

Traditional puppet performances are playful, comic recreations of old, sometimes ancient texts and mingle with these ancient texts new humorous episodes and interludes. Examples are numerous. Antonio Pasqualino demonstrates that when Orlando of the *Song of Roland* becomes crazy, he behaves like Pulcinella of the commedia dell'arte. Joan Gross shows that when Tchantchès interacts with Charlemagne, a nineteenth-twentieth century peasant-worker meets with a medieval king. As discussed in the paper by Frederik E. deBoer, when Balinese clowns translate the noble-gods of the *Mahabharata* and the *Ramayana*, ancient India mingles with modern Indonesia. These mingled texts, which cut across time and space, are the meeting place of popular, traditional, folk, high, and elite culture. The resulting exuberant language and content is a source of great humor for audiences, which appreciate both the congruent and the incongruent mixes.

The satirical parody of social rules and social boundaries characteristic of puppetry constitutes a subversion of social structure and especially a comic attack on the hegemonic role of the dominating class, which, of course, is represented culturally by what each society considers its high culture. Finally puppets make and break frames, reminding spectators of the arbitrariness and fragility of what is the definition of what is going on at the moment.[6]

As pointed out by all of the authors, changing audiences for puppet performances have resulted in differences in shared expectations and understandings of underlying comic codes and led to differing interpretations and reactions. Antonio Pasqualino in particular discusses how different Sicilian social classes respond in different ways to the humor and comedy of the *pupi*. In western Europe in particular, puppets, which have their origins in popular, lower, and working class settings, especially epitomized by the fair ground and the carnival, have become more and more of a middle class phenomenon. As a result they have lost much of their satirical bite and are considered most appropriate for children and for museums.

The papers in this collection, which deal with forms of puppetry from the native American Southwest to villages in Java and Bali, Indonesia, demonstrate the variety and individuality of forms of puppet humor, as well as certain general and shared characteristics. These papers utilize classic theories of humor, such as those of Bergson, Baudelaire, and Freud, but at the same time demonstrate the relevance of studies of puppetry for a general understanding of the nature of comedy and humor. Each of the authors is a specialist in her/his area of the world and has carried out extensive field research. The authors intimately know the society and culture in which the puppet traditions which they analyze are a part. In addition they make use of concepts from anthropology, folklore, linguistics, semiotics, and drama and literary criticism.

The papers are organized from more general to more specific. Antonio Pasqualino, "Humor and puppets," while focusing on the Italian puppet traditions he has researched in considerable depth, explores the general nature of humor in puppets. Frank Proschan, "The cocreation of the comic in puppetry," deals with a quite widespread source of humor in puppetry, interactions with the audience, relating his general knowledge of this area to an examination of particular performances of *Punch and Judy*. Drawing on a variety of puppet traditions from around the world, Dina and Joel Sherzer, "Verbal humor in the puppet theater," deal with the role of language in puppet humor and comedy. Kathy Foley, "The clown figure in the puppet theater of West Java: the ancestor and the individual," deals with a rich and complex ongoing glove puppet tradition, the Javanese *wayang golek*. She focuses on the clowns, their origins, developments, behaviors, and satirical roles in modern, changing Indonesia. Frederik E. deBoer, who is a specialist on Indonesian theater, offers a detailed presentation of the various comic techniques of the four comic attendants (the *panasar*) in a Balinese *wayang kulit* (shadowplay) performance. His paper shows concretely how various semiotic systems are made to work together to create comic effects; it highlights the complicated and sophisticated performance of the *dalang* (puppeteer) and points to the roots of humor in Balinese village life today against the backdrop of ancient tradition. Joan Gross, "The form and function of humor in the Liège puppet theater," studies the rod puppets of Liège, Belgium, a tradition closely linked to the Sicilian *pupi* discussed by Antonio Pasqualino. She examines the various forms of humor in this tradition and their relation to the changing role of puppetry in Belgian society. Jane Young, "Humor and anti-humor in Western Puebloan puppetry performances," examines Hopi and Zuni Indian puppet traditions. Puppet performances occur in the context of the annual cycle of sacred dramas and are an important aspect of their ritual. Like so many other puppet traditions, Western Puebloan puppets both support and challenge the world view of the society and culture in which they are performed. They enact carnivalesque rituals of reversal, which invert what is ordinarily considered appropriate behavior.

A number of themes and questions cut across the particular papers and topics in this volume. Are puppets inherently comical? What is the general function of puppet humor, social critique or a letting off of social steam? In complex societies, especially those with stratified class structures, what are the different humorous messages puppets express? Can they be humorous for one group and serious for another, or humorous for different groups in different ways? How does the nature of puppet humor change over time as the role of the puppet theater changes, from a popular to a middle class phenomenon, from the fair ground to the museum, the library, and the public school? What kinds of humorous relationships emerge from the interplay of past and present, as when contemporary Belgian, Indonesian, Italian, and Western Puebloan audiences watch enactments of ancient epics? One intriguing question which Antonio Pasqualino raises in his paper and which is relevant to all the papers is how seriously to take how seriously traditional audiences seem to take puppetry? The answer to this question involves an understanding of the mixture of seriousness and humor and of closeness and distance and irony which is at the heart of puppetry.

It is our hope that this collection of papers, together with a growing scholarly literature dealing with puppetry and other forms of expressive culture which involve people looking at and reframing themselves and their social lives, will contribute to an understanding of the significance of puppetry as a form of popular culture and to an appreciation of its exuberance and vitality.

Notes

[1] See Frank Proschan, ed. *Puppets, Masks and Performing Objects from Semiotic Perspectives* (*Semiotica* 47(1/4), 1983).

[2] See for example Cyril Beaumont, *Puppets and Puppetry* (New York: The Studio Publications, 1958); Paul Fournel, ed., *Les Marionnettes* (Paris: Bordas, 1982); Michael R. Malkin, *Traditional and Folk Puppets of the World* (New York: A.S. Barnes and Co., 1977); René Simmen, *The World of Puppets* (New York: Thomas Y. Crowell, 1972); and George Speaight, *The History of the English Puppet Theater* (New York: John de Graff, 1955).

[3] See Alton L. Becker, "Text-building, epistemology, and aesthetics in Javanese Shadow Theater," in *The Imagination of Reality*, ed. by Alton L. Becker and Aram Yengoyan (Norwood, New Jersey: Ablex Publishing, 1979), pp. 211-243; James R. Brandon, ed., *On Thrones of Gold: Three Javanese Shadow Plays* (Cambridge: Harvard University Press, 1970); Hedi Hinzler, *Bima Swarga in Balinese Wayang* (Verhandelingen van het Koninklijk Instituut voor Taal-,Land-en Volkenkunde 90) (The Hague: Martinus Nijhoff, 1981); Ward Keeler, *Javanese Shadow Plays* (Princeton: Princeton University Press, 1987); Colin McPhee, "The Balinese Wayang Kulit and its Music," *Djawa* 16 (1936) pp. 1-34; Amin Sweeney, *The Ramayana and the Malay Shadow Play* (Kuala Lumpur: National University of Malaysia Press, 1972); H. Ulbricht, *Wayang Purwa: Shadows of the Past* (Kuala Lumpur: Oxford University Press, 1970); and Mary Zurbuchen, *The Shadow Theater of Bali: Explorations in language and text.* (Princeton: Princeton University Press, 1987).

[4] See papers in Proschan (1983).

[5] See Keeler; Katharine Luomala, *Hula Ki'i: Hawaiian Puppetry* (Honolulu: Institute for Polynesian Studies, 1984); Antonio Pasqualino, *L'Opera dei Pupi* (Palermo: Sellerio editore, 1977); Proschan (1983); Frank Proschan, "Puppet Voices and Interlocutors: Language in Folk Puppetry," *Journal of American Folklore*, 94 (1981), pp. 527-555; and Zurbuchen.

[6] Erving Goffman's *Frame Analysis* (New York: Harper and Row, 1974) is a most relevant source for the concept of frame.

Humor and Puppets: an Italian Perspective

Antonio Pasqualino

In the puppet theater the relationship between comic and dramatic effects is revealed in all its complexities and ambiguities. Puppets, like live human actors, are used in both comic and serious plays, and the latter often have humorous characters. But puppets are often considered to be particularly appropriate for the performance of comic plays; and often serious puppet plays are considered to be humorous and are appreciated as such.

Using as its primary example the puppet tradition of southern Italy, this paper will discuss the expression of the comic in puppets, focusing on the mechanisms used in this expression; comic subjects, situations, and actions in the puppet theater and the mechanisms based on content;[1] and, finally, three closely related problems: (1) the inherent humor of puppets, that is, whether puppets are especially appropriate for the comic and are felt to be comic even if they are intended to enact a serious plot; (2) the misunderstanding of a serious play as humorous by spectators who do not share and understand the cultural assumptions of the performance; and (3) the coexistence of serious and humorous appreciation of a performance by a traditional audience.

Two types of puppet show are widespread in continental southern Italy and Sicily: the *guarattelle*, glove puppets which represent the vicissitudes of Pulcinella, and the *opera dei pupi*, marionettes manipulated from above with iron rods and representing chivalrous subjects.[2]

In Italy the traditional comic characters of the glove puppet shows, those of the *opera dei pupi*, and those of the marionette theater are the old masked characters of the *Commedia dell'Arte* and the characters that appeared at the beginning of the nineteenth century. The word "masked" indicates fixed theatrical types. The old masked characters actually wear masks to cover their faces. The new characters, although very similar to the old masked characters, do not. In the marionette theater, both

8

became well behaved symbols of urban working class respectability, while in the glove puppet shows they remained violent, rebellious peasants, with disquieting traces of their descent from the demons of the agrarian fertility rites.

Today both glove puppet and *opera dei pupi* shows are performed for audiences interested in traditional culture, under conditions very different from those of the past. Traditionally, the *guarattelle* were used in the simplest form of street performance, a poor people's amusement, although recommended also for rich children. The performance presents the almost invariably victorious struggles of Pulcinella against a number of antagonists, neighbors, authorities, and supernatural beings, and shows him playing with corpses, dying and resurrecting, and giving birth to many small Pulcinellas. The hero of the *guarattelle*, like the Pulcinella of Carnival, is an ambiguous personage, with a polymorphous sexuality, who assumes contradictory meanings connected with the ideas of death, birth, and rebirth.

In the glove puppet shows of northern Italy the audience was also the very low social orders. The plot is often more complex, a story of adventures with wicked tyrants and innocent victims, that constantly mixes the comic with drama. The masked character is always there, as main hero or as helper of the hero, and it is usually the masked character who performs the heroic action that restores justice. The audience of the *opera dei pupi* was popular or, at the very most, lower middle class. The subject, the epic of the Paladins of France, fighting against a foreign enemy, the Saracens, and a domestic threat, the traitors, portrays and ennobles the ideology of the audience by means of a series of misunderstandings.[3] Comical scenes were interwoven together with the scenes that were supposed to represent history. In these comical scenes, the masked characters appeared playing the role of servants of the heroes. At the end of the play, farces were performed, in which the masked characters were the main characters.

In the *opera dei pupi* and in the more complex glove puppet performances, the masked characters, Nofriu, Virticchiu, Gioppino, Fagiolino, and Pulcinella, often display a behavior that, more or less in keeping with the romantic or fabulous vicissitudes of the plot, is identical with that of the Pulcinella of the *guarattelle*.

The expression of the comic in puppets

In a comic puppet show the state of the audience, expecting something humorous, is very important. As Freud expresses it:

The favorable condition for the origin of comic pleasure is brought about by a general happy disposition in which "one is in the mood for laughing."... A similar favorable condition is produced by the expectation of the comic, or by putting one's self in the right mood for comic pleasure...He who decides to attend a comic lecture or a farce at the theater is indebted to this intention for laughing over things which in his everyday life would hardly produce in him a comic effect. He finally laughs at the recollection of having laughed, at the expectation of laughing, and at the appearance of the one who is to present the comic, even before the latter makes the attempt to make him laugh.[4]

Thus all of the expressive elements of a comic puppet show, the language, the characteristics of the voice, and the movements of the puppets and their figurative grotesque features, are apt to provoke laughter in the audience, even before the plot, situation, and actions are appreciated as comic.

It should also be noted that, in a show which has both serious and comic parts, such as the *opera dei pupi*, the Belgian marionettes, and the Javenese or Balinese *wayang*, the serious and comic personages differ in their use of the various expressive codes.[5] All the elements of the comic expressive codes, apart from their ability to produce laughter by means of the technique of expression and by means of content, function as a signal of the comic, in opposition to the corresponding serious elements, switching the expectations and mood of the audience.

The linguistic codes of the *guarattelle* have only the comic register. The language of Pulcinella and most other personages is Neapolitan dialect, or, outside the Campania region, a mixture of Neapolitan and the local dialect. Personages of a high social order, such as judges and doctors, frequently use garbled Italian. The priest is often caricatured by making him speak pig latin.

The linguistic codes of the *opera dei pupi* have two registers, one comic, prevalently in Sicilian dialect, and one heroic, in literary Italian.[6] This corresponds to a general practice of Italian theater. In acting, conforming to a tradition going back to the sixteenth century and still observed today by comic actors in the theater, in the movies, and on television, Italian is used for serious characters of high social position and local dialects for comic characters and poor people. Comic characters are mostly poor. Comic characters of high social class often speak either dialectal or garbled Italian.

Two reasons can be given for this linguistic usage in relation to the comic. (1) Joking and humor are felt to be inappropriate for official occasions and appropriate for familiar situations. For this reason they are more appropriately expressed in everyday language. (2) Since official symbols and occasions become comic when their rules are subverted and degraded, the language that is used on official occasions becomes comic when it is subverted and degraded. Compared to the official language, the local language is felt to be not a communication system in its own right, but an alteration equivalent to garbled Italian and pig latin, an imperfect expression of the uneducated. Something very similar can happen with foreign languages.[7]

The comic characters of the *opera dei pupi* speak Sicilian or use other regional accents and dialects of their supposed home town. An innkeeper in Rome speaks Roman, the Neapolitan Testuzza speaks Neapolitan, or garbled Italian.

Traditionally, the heroic characters were supposed and assumed to speak ancient Italian, modelled on fourteenth and sixteenth century poems, sources of the *Storia dei paladini di Francia*, a novel by Giusto Lodico used by the puppeteers. In actuality, these characters spoke a mixture of this literary language and of contemporary regional Italian and Sicilian. This linguistic mixture was interpreted as serious by the usual audience, but appeared comic to upper class spectators, who did not share the *opera dei pupi* communicative conventions.[8]

Much of the speech of the comic characters involves playing with words and uttering absurd statements, free from the constraints of linguistic and rational rules, similar in some ways to the playful verbal activities that occupy and amuse children at the time when they learn to speak.[9]

There are also characteristics of the voice which are specifically comic. The timbre of Pulcinella's voice is altered by the use of a swazzle that makes it strident, so that words are difficult to understand. The inarticulate sounds produced by the puppeteer's voice include the raspberries with which Pulcinella announces his entry and punctuates his speech, an allusion to bodily functions excluded from polite conversation.

In the *opera dei pupi* the timbre of the voice changes with the type of character and distinguishes the positive comic ones, the negative comic ones, the positive serious ones, and the negative serious ones. The positive comic characters, the masked characters, speak with nasal, clucking, and raucous voices, different from the negative comic characters, such as the Saracen Ferraù, who speaks dialect with a throaty, strident voice, and Gano di Maganza, the traitor, who is also, strangely enough, a comic character, and also has a strident, clucking, nasal voice, which at times turns falsetto. The positive heroes have a clear, resounding timbre; the negative ones, an obscure, throaty, and raucous one. Both in the glove puppets and in the *opera dei pupi*, the strident or falsetto voice used by a male person is comic because it is feminine and childish and alludes to a sexual ambiguity. The raucous voice is, on the other hand, an exaggerated male voice.

The rhythm of the speech of the comic characters is fast and uniform; the rhythm of the speech of the heroic characters is slower, speeding up and slowing down to stress the emotions, with pauses of variable duration. Vibrato, a frequent feature of the voice of serious characters, which stresses highly emotional states, is never found in the voices of the comic characters. Appreciated by traditional audiences, as an artistic virtuosity of the puppeteer's performance, it may appear exaggerated and humorous to the irregular spectator.

The imitation of sounds is also humorous. The puppeteer uses his voice to imitate snoring, yawning, and the smacking sound of kisses, making the audience laugh because of the way in which he exaggerates the real sounds which serve as his model.

Special sounds punctuate puppet performances, emphasizing speech, movements, and gestures. In the *guarattelle*, there is the knocking of the cudgels or of the puppets' heads against each other or against the front board; in the *opera dei pupi*, there is the wooden sound produced by the stomping of the puppeteer's clogs on the floor boards that resounds like a drum, or the metallic sound obtained by hitting the metal maneuvering rods against a metal bar on which the puppets can be hanged. These sounds have fast and uniform rhythms when punctuating comic speech; rapid rhythms with jerks and jumps when marking comic movements; slower rhythms, often speeding up and slowing down, when punctuating serious, dramatic, tragic speech; slow, relatively constant rhythm when marking the movement of serious characters. In Indonesia, a rhythmical sound, an aspect of the musical structure of the gamelan music which is integrated with the puppet performance, is produced by the puppeteer with a foot hammer that hits either the side of the box which holds the puppets, producing a wooden sound similar to that of the Sicilian clogs, or some metal plates hanging on the side of the puppet box, producing a metallic sound similar to that of the Sicilian rods. These sounds are also used for giving orders concerning the music, in Sicily to start or stop it, in Indonesia, in addition, to indicate what music should be played.

Humor is also produced by the features of the puppets, by their movements and gestures, and by their relation to the scenic space. In the world of the *guarattelle*, where everything is comic, all the movements and gestures, characterized by strong and even rhythms, are comic. Compared to the ordinary movements of humans, they appear exaggerated and similar to a repetitive dance rhythm. The movements of fights are a prime example. The puppets clash cudgels, hit the enemy's heads many times, alternate hitting the weapons and the heads of the enemy, fall on stage and get up, and grab a fallen body and swing it in front of the stage or throw it away.

Glove puppets also bang their heads on the stage, carry a coffin on their shoulders, climb on a wing of the stage, and play with corpses, arranging and rearranging them in heaps of different shapes, placing them in coffins, and turning them around and knocking them in with their heads. They walk around, showing fear or self assurance; show off like street bullies, walking proudly and swaying their hips; and show excitement by banging their foreheads on the stage or extreme surprise by jumping and falling backwards, banging the back of their heads on the stage. They also show a comic aggressiveness by butting someone with their heads, by directing their backsides at someone while giving vent to a vulgar sound, by stretching one arm toward someone while putting their other hand under or on top if it, or by stretching out their stomachs toward someone. These gestures are intentionally comic; that is, the puppet that uses them is understood to be intending to be comic. The fact that they allude symbolically to sexual aggression contributes to their comical effect.

In the *opera dei pupi* there are both comic and vulgar poses, movements, and gestures and serious and noble ones. The former are used by the comic characters and the latter by the serious ones. At the same time there are exceptions, such as when serious characters assume comic poses, to be discussed below. It is considered comic to express satisfaction by shaking oneself with one's knees slightly bent or to express happiness by jumping with one's feet together or with one leg raised. It is also considered comic to show surprise by jumping with both feet as it is to express fear by scratching one's head, while trembling. To run into a stage wing, as Saracen soldiers and ambassadors often do when leaving the stage, is an exaggerated comic expression of fear and confusion. It is an interesting question whether in the heroic world of the *opera dei pupi* fear is a comic element in and of itself, so that all expressions of fear are comic. In fact, the heroes, when they are in a hopeless situation, do not show fear by trembling. Rather they express desperation by means of a vibrato voice, what the puppeteers call *lamento*. On the other hand, females or old people can be afraid without being comic. Fear is comic when expressed by a character who, because of his status, is supposed not to be afraid. Other gestures performed by the masked characters of the *opera dei pupi* are, as in the case of glove puppets, intentional comic expressions of symbolic sexual aggression.

Gestures that are not in themselves noble or vulgar can take on these connotations because of the speed and rhythm of their execution. There are three styles of movements. (1) Serious: slow with constant rhythm, for instance walking in a slow and staid manner. (2) Merry: rapid movements with changeable rhythm, for instance, fast steps stopping and starting again vivaciously. (3) Comic and unrefined: rapid

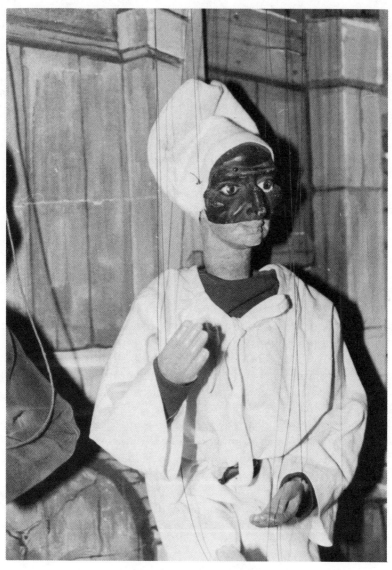

Italian string puppet *Pulcinella*
Photo: A. Pasqualino

Italian string puppet *Arlecchino*
Photo: A. Pasqualino

Glove puppet from Sicily *Pulcinella*
Photo: A. Pasqualino

Sicilian puppets
Comic figures: (from the left) *Nofriu, Virticchiu, Lisa, Testuzza*
Photo: A. Pasqualino

movements with jerks and jumps, for instance, walking fast or jerkily or walking with skipping movements. These movements are interpreted as exaggerated and incongruous by the audience. But all the movements and gestures, serious as well as noble, and especially those that emphasize speech, such as stepping backward and forward, constantly moving the head from left to right and vice versa, are potentially comic for spectators who do not share the conventions of the *opera dei pupi* system.

The same can be said for the movements of battles. In fact, the various movements of *pupi* battles are very similar to those of the glove puppets. They are also symmetrical and repetitive, with rhythm that gets faster and faster. But in serious scenes, these movements are not felt by the audience to be comic, but rather highly dramatic. The battles are expected to be the most exciting part of the performance. Here is where the qualities of the puppeteer as a virtuoso are judged. In their discussion and praise of the fight dance of the puppets, enthusiastic audiences and puppeteers go so far as identifying artistic qualities of battles in realistic terms. A comic character fights with a very slow rhythm, at times suddenly speeding up. This is considered very amusing and elicits laughter from the audience.

Because of the way they fly, swinging to and fro from one side to the other of the stage, and the way they speak, with a falsetto voice (the voice of a child), angels, who are serious for traditional audiences, are comic for outsiders.

These contrasts in the way traditional and non-traditional audiences interpret and react to puppet performances bring us back to the question of expectations as key to an understanding of audience reactions. Expectations are determined by artistic conventions and assumptions. At the same time, it can be noted that movements and gestures are usually comic because they appear exaggerated and incongruous, as well as because of meanings that they encode.

The physical appearance of the comic puppets is characterized by particular features. The masked characters of the glove puppet show and those of the *opera dei pupi*'s farces and comic scenes wear contemporary costumes or the special costumes that traditional iconography attributes to them. They appear comic because they are strangely rough, because some of their features are exaggerated, or, in the *opera dei pupi*'s epics, because they are in a completely different fashion from the costumes of the serious characters. Arlecchino and Gianduia have enormous warts, Fagiolino has three enormous goiters, Virticchiu has an asymmetrical face, such as is produced by paralysis of the facial nerve, and Testuzza has an enormous head.[10]

The masked characters are all of small stature compared to the heroes. In addition the comic representative of evil, the traitor Gano di Maganza, is of small stature and has a scar on his face. The small stature of the comic characters can be related to the small stature of children who the masked characters resemble also in the way they break rules of politeness in social interaction. Recognizing the behavior of a child in an adult is one of the basic techniques of the comic.[11] Perceiving that heroes are of small stature compared to humans is one of the mechanisms that can transform a serious scene into a comic one, leading to the sense that puppets are always comic, no matter what they do. (See further discussion below).

The serious characters in the *opera dei pupi* are grouped into positive and negative types. The positive have gentle and noble features; the negative, coarse and brutal faces. The latter can often be seen as comic, setting up in the audience an expectation of comic behavior from the enemies. They display extravagant ferocity, overconfidence, and fear.

The rules that govern the cooccurrence and coherence of the various linguistic and non-linguistic elements that are manifested by each character type in the *opera dei pupi* are rigid. Puppeteers say that they cannot, for instance, move a puppet or make it speak in a way that contrasts with its face or clothing. Thus they cannot give a brutal voice to a puppet that has a gentle face, or give a noble facial expression and behavior to a comic puppet.[12] Nevertheless, in particular circumstances, as mentioned above, serious characters can move in a comic manner.

All of the characters in the *guarattelle* and the comic characters in the *opera dei pupi* take great liberties with the usual conventions of ordinary, human theater. They climb on wings and screech out from the top of the theatrical structure. The breach of rules of the conventional stage, a significant aspect of the frame of the performance, is a source of the comic in the puppet theater. But if a serious character in a serious scene climbs on a wing, as might exceptionally happen, he is not playing with the frame of the performance. In this case, the action is interpreted realistically by the puppeteer and by the audience as climbing up some real thing that has to be imagined in accord with the suggestions of the dialog, although not represented by an item of the scenery, e.g. a wall or a tree.

The participation of the audience in the *guarattelle* and other glove puppet shows is continually provoked by the puppeteer with questions that the puppets ask and with requests for help or advice. The conversation of a puppet with a member of the audience is an occasion for playing with words, but is also a source of comic for other reasons. It draws the attention of the audience to some of its members, exposing them, if they do not react properly, to a loss of face. And it breaks the frame of the performance and exposes it as false and artificial, thus deflating the puppeteer's pretention of creating an illusive world. In the *opera dei pupi* as well there are intrusions of some members of the audience into the performance, to protect a hero in danger or, to support him, to attack an enemy or a traitor, or to control the excessive boasting of a character. All of these actions are comic, the latter overtly so and the former with a combination of utmost seriousness and auto-irony.

The content of the puppet theater: serious and comic

The *guarattelle* show consists of a series of encounters between the protagonist Pulcinella and neighbors, various representatives of the social order—the doctor, the policeman, the judge, the priest, and the hangman, and various supernatural beings—death and the devil. Pulcinella ends up by fighting them and is almost invariably the winner. He plays with corpses. He is sometimes killed and comes back to life. He eats enormously. In the end he usually obtains a nice girl for a fiancée, but can also become pregnant and give birth to many small Pulcinellas.

Pulcinella is seen as a poor man, so that when he makes fun of the powerful he gives satisfaction to a feeling of social rebellion. But he can also be seen as a child, because he is small and behaves like a child. Finally he is like some kind of supernatural being representing life or death. This third identification is suggested by the following facts— he resuscitates himself, he is dressed in white, color of death, he is sexually ambiguous, and his beak nose and peculiar voice make him resemble a bird, the word bird (*uccello*) being used to refer to the male sexual organ.

Pulcinella's adventures touch some of the wishes that are restrained and repressed by society, common topics of the comic in general. These are: (1) innocent comic: the pleasure of playing with words and sounds, without caring about their logical or rational meaning. (2) Sexual comic: Pulcinella's exaggerated and ambiguous sexual behavior, including representing himself as a sexual organ and joking about sex and bodily excretions and breaking the ordinary rules of behavior concerning these activities. (3) Aggressive comic: the expression of an unrestrained aggressiveness—the caricaturing, unmasking, and degrading of characters and Pulcinella's punishing with death, without moral or effective social consequences, all those who oppose him. Identifying themselves with him, the spectators enjoy a sort of delirium of unlimited power. (4) Cynical comic: caricature, unmasking and degradation of personages who, because of their status and because they represent the institutions of the state and the church, are supposed to have the right to authority and command respect—the policeman, the judge, and the priest. In addition, playing with death and the ordinary rules of behavior with regard to death is a sort of negation of society. Fighting the devil as Pulcinella does is, in a sense, a blasphemous negation of religion.[13] In general, the *guarattelle* constitute an indistinct universe, animated by elementary instincts and needs, in which Pulcinella requires no justification for his murderous rites.

In the more complex glove puppet plays of northern Italy, the same comic scenes occur, in a universe that has undergone a division into good and evil, in the culminating moments of an adventurous plot that exalts noble ideals. It is the masked character who kills the wicked enemy and liberates the princess, and it is precisely in doing this that he behaves exactly like the Pulcinella of the *guarattelle*—fighting with his cudgel and heaping up and playing with corpses.

In the *opera dei pupi* the distinction between good and evil is as sharp and the distinction between comic and serious is sharper than that in the glove puppet plays of northern Italy, the serious portion of the performance being larger and much more developed. The story of Charlemagne and his knights was performed in installments and lasted more than a year. It expresses a great aggressiveness in the fights, ending with heaps of corpses and dismembering of enemies. This rite of death is justified by a complex political-religious ideology, opposing, in a long and complex plot, good and evil, just and diabolic religion, loyalty and disloyalty, Christians and Saracens, and converts and traitors.

The comic, masked characters of the *opera dei pupi*, both those who appear in the farces that follow the main performance, and those who appear in the comic scenes interwoven with the serious plot, are very similar to the masked characters of the glove puppet show, except that they usually do not do the killing themselves. This they leave to the serious heroes. But once the heap of corpses is there, they often jump on it with a raised leg, or sit on it. These comic scenes are not found in the written sources of the puppeteers; they derive from a theatrical tradition which introduces the masked characters into all kinds of plots.

But, in addition, the serious portion of the *opera dei pupi*, the plot of the adventures of Charlemagne and his knights, is not completely serious, either in performances or in most of its sources.[14] The main comic element in all the comic situations of the chivalrous plot is caricature, unmasking, and degradation. The behavior of many of the Saracens, kings, warriors, giants, and soldiers involves some comic traits. These occur when they boast or are afraid, so that comic and negative values are often associated. The giant Ferraù, who is coarse and speaks Sicilian, even has long comic scenes. The devil of the magical scenes, waving his tail, is comic as a mixture of human and animal features.[15] Strangely enough, Gano di Maganza, the traitor, the character that traditional audiences hated and tried to destroy, is, as we have noted, a comic figure, resembling the masked characters in his voice, stature, facial markings, and behavior. He shows fear and jumps with a raised leg on the corpses of the dead heroes who he has betrayed and assassinated, just like the masked characters jump on the corpses of the dead enemies. Among the Christian heroes, Astolfo, who boasts more than he can accomplish, is comic.

Charlemagne and Orlando become comic only at certain moments. Charlemagne is comic when he is rebuked in his tyrannical behavior. Orlando is comic when he is a naive child growing up in the woods, when he is a naive lover, when he can be suspected of being sexually unfit, and when he becomes mad because of love. Derision of Charlemagne is derision of the state; derision of Orlando is derision of a model of self. The blindness of tyrants and madness are typical comic subjects, the latter more spectacularly so. It is manifested by a concentration of nonsensical and childish behavior and a loss of rational control of actions and words, as well as a loss of the rules of decency concerning sex and excretions and of respect for other individuals, to the point of endangering their lives. When Orlando becomes mad, this noble hero throws away his armor and runs naked in the woods. He mistakes Nofriu, the masked character who follows him faithfully as his servant, for Angelica, the princess who has refused his love, and urinates on him. He kills everybody he meets, so that we might say that he has reverted to the behavior of Pulcinella of the *guarattelle*.

It might seem appropriate to identify the comic that is found within the chivalrous narrative of the *opera dei pupi* as "minor" and the comic of the masked characters as "major," in the sense that Bataille has given to these terms. The former, similar to the "meaningful comic" of Baudelaire, circulates commonly in everyday life; with it society strengthens itself and excludes what appears peripheral, inadequate to the central values of the culture. The latter, the carnivalesque type of humor, similar to the "absolute comic" of Baudelaire, starts from below, and subverts the pretensions to perfection of the center, its authority and ideology.[16] The comic aspects of Saracens and of Astolfo are of the "minor" type. But some of the elements of the comic in the epic plots— Charlemagne degraded to an old fool, Orlando the most perfect hero being transformed into Pulcinella, Gano di Maganza presented as a perverse version of Pulcinella in contrast to the positive masked characters—must be considered as rooted in the culture of Carnival and therefore "major comic."

The inherent humor of puppets, humor through misunderstanding, the coexistence of serious and humorous appreciation of a performance

As we have noted, puppets are often considered to be not only especially appropriate for the performance of comic plays, but inherently comic, in and of themselves. In addition, serious puppets may often be perceived as ridiculous or parodistic in two different situations: (1) The serious intention of the puppeteer is transformed in its reception, by an audience that does not share the specific codes and understanding of the traditional puppeteer and his audience. (2) Serious puppets are occasionally perceived as humorous also by a traditional audience. This can happen with all sorts of artistic mimesis, as Bergson noted, although perhaps more often with puppets.[17]

The idea that puppets are especially appropriate for the comic can be linked to two theses. The first is Bergson's definition of the comic as the effect produced by the discovery of mechanical and repetitive features in life, since, according to this French philosopher, life is governed by the rule of never repeating itself.[18] The second emerges from the fact that puppets, compared to humans, are small, like children, and when they behave seriously, they are, like children, pretending to be adults. It is also related to the fact that puppets are for children.[19] It is not easy to indicate when this began. At the beginning of the nineteenth century it was common in France and not yet in Italy.[20]

Magnin and other scholars considered puppets not only especially appropriate for the comic, but also inherently parodistic.[21] Magnin also noted that puppets could be perceived as either comic or, since they simulate life, as strange, the effect of witchcraft, or magic. This idea can be traced to the "second Romanticism."[22]

This double image of puppets (as comic or as strange or magical) has led to discussions among students of the puppet theater, for example that opposing Zich and Bogatyrev in the 1920's.[23] Zich describes the comic and the strange or magical as two poles in the way puppets can be perceived, the effects they can produce. If the audience perceives them as inanimate objects, then the potential for puppets to be mistaken for living beings produces a comic or grotesque effect. If on the other hand the audience perceives them as living beings, then their fixed faces and the rigidity and anatomical peculiarities of their movements produce the sensation of something wonderful, unexplainable, and enigmatic, i.e. strange and magical. This point of view is rooted in the comparison of puppets with live, human actors and in the observation that serious forms of string puppet performances, like many European traditional folk forms, had a kind of magical appeal for their traditional audiences, but could appear as a parody of live, human theater to a cultivated audience.

Bogatyrev criticized Zich's evaluation of the puppet theater, stressing that all artistic products can be perceived either as signs belonging to their own system or as material objects, the latter if we concentrate our attention on the signifiers without relating them to the signifieds. Doing so distorts perception, as when the signs of one system are perceived in the terms of another system, for instance when people laugh at a language they do not understand, misinterpreting the sentences as garbled forms of a familiar language. Only an audience that knows how to "read" it can properly understand the text of a performance.[24]

To understand the point of this dispute we must recall the Czech situation which both Zich and Bogatyrev had in mind. There were two types of puppet theater, with audiences of different social and cultural backgrounds, a serious, dramatic folk theater and an emerging, cultivated, avant garde theater. The latter had two trends, one humorous and the other symbolic and mysterious.[25] The dramatic scenes of the Czech folk theater, like those of the Sicilian *opera dei pupi*, often appeared ridiculous to cultivated audiences that did not understand their style.

Pitrè writes of the *opera dei pupi*: "To enthusiasts of the *opra* everything appears serious and solemn, even that which is overtly parodic."[26] However, Pitrè himself, and cultivated individuals whose interest for the *opera dei pupi* was aroused by his writings, could integrate in their perception of the play the comic effects created by the internal social disparities of Italian culture with the serious emotion of the everyday spectators, whereas for most educated people the comic perception caused disregard and disdain. This is of course one of the ways that elites express their power and demonstrate their consciousness of it.

According to Jurkowski, Zich's concern was the modern puppet theater that he hoped would evolve a strong style in one of the two directions suggested by the nature of puppets, either comic or symbolic.[27] But Bogatyrev thought that Zich's attitude was similar to that of the bourgeois public when confronted with folk theater. Bogatyrev was right to say that the live, human actors' theater and the puppet theater are different semiotic systems. But it should also be said that neither is a fixed system. Both change in space and time. So an audience accustomed to a certain type of theater may be unprepared for another type and unable to understand it. Differences between the intentions of a performer and the reception by an audience may efface the artistic value of a performance.

But differences between sender and receiver competence are a common feature of the communicative process. Reception of an artistic performance requires the knowledge of specific sign systems, but does not exclude comparisons with reality and with other sign systems. All systems have traces of other systems belonging to the same culture and of that particular semiotic construct which we call reality. This is a normal feature of culture in general and also of theater. So Zich's comparison of puppet theater with live actors' theater and of puppets with humans is not only legitimate for the student of theater, but is a normal aspect of the audience perception of the puppet theater.

A fitting example of this double, comic and serious, perception of the Sicilian puppet theater is found in a travelogue written in the beginning of this century by Henry Festing Jones.[28] Whereas most travelers describe this curious item of local culture borrowing Pitrè's words, Jones repeatedly visited several theaters, observed with attention, asked for explanations, and took notes. He had the taste of a real theatergoer and an exceptional ability to participate in an esthetic experience based on rules and conventions different from those of the official European theater. Jones was not insensitive to the comic effects created by these differences; rather he noted them with amusement. But he was also able to create a contact with the people who accompanied him and with the puppeteers. This allowed him to participate in the pathos and drama, perceiving the mixture of comedy and tragedy.

The idea that the puppet folk theater is naively interpreted as serious by its usual audience and as comic by educated and sophisticated spectators is overly simplistic. Of course educated audiences sometimes perceive as comic scenes that the traditional folk audience interpret as serious. But the opposite happens as well, as when lower class spectators laugh at aspects of cultivated performances that are serious for their usual audiences. Within the rules of every artistic performance there are large possibilities for serious and comic perceptions to alternate. The rules provide a framework for interpreting some things as comic and others as serious. But they also suggest possibilities for distantiation that may transform even the most serious texts in a comic direction.[29] The possibilities of transforming drama into comedy are exploited to a greater or lesser degree by the audience, and might even remain unexploited, but they are an integral part of all artistic activities. For this reason, a spectator coming from another cultural world can either refuse to understand or else enter the game that the rules provide and integrate within it the effects created by cultural distance.

The traditional audiences of the *opera dei pupi* did not laugh only at the openly comic aspects of the show. A great emotional participation in the dramatic aspects of the performance did not prevent a good measure of irony and auto-irony. To take too seriously the expressions of joy and sorrow, love and hatred, on the part of the traditional audience of the *opera dei pupi*, that have been described many times, gives a false and absurd image of it. Quarreling about whether Orlando is stronger

than Rinaldo or vice versa, paying the puppeteer to set a prisoner hero
free, exhibiting great sorrow for the death of a hero, showing one's hatred
for the traitors trying to destroy the puppets were not acts of madness,
but ways of participating consciously in the play, in the illusion of the
spectacle. Such apparently spontaneous episodes were repeated over and
over again by different people in different times and places. The
interventions of the spectators were actually elements of the performance,
anticipated by the rules, actualized in an aleatory way and at will by
some spectators. Alongside behavior that demonstrates passionate
participation, others, that have been reported in many different places
and times, are ironic and polemic exchanges with the puppeteer, thus
reducing the epic hyperboles characteristic of the *opera dei pupi*.[30]

Notes

[1]See Sigmund Freud, "Wit and its relation to the unconscious," in *The Basic
Writings of Sigmund Freud*, translated and edited by A.A. Brill (New York: The
Modern Library, 1938), pp. 631-803, especially the last section, VII. "Wit and the
various forms of the comic" (pp. 762-803). See also Giulio Ferroni, *ll comico nelle
teorie contemporanee*, (Rome: Bulzoni, 1974), pp. 74-77.

[2]*Guarattella* is Neapolitan, corresponding to the Sicilian *tutui*, Milanese *megatel*,
and Italian *burattino*. *Pupo* in southern Italy means puppet (but also doll, statuette);
it is used now to distinguish the rod puppet manipulated from above from the
marionetta (string puppet) and the *burattino* (glove puppet). The Italian glove puppets
are very similar to the English Punch, the Russian Petrushka, the Czechoslovakian
Kasparek, and the Egyptian Aragoz.

[3]Antonio Pasqualino, *L'Opera dei Pupi* (Palermo: Sellerio editore, 1977).

[4]Freud, p. 790.

[5]Pasqualino (1977) and "Marionettes and glove puppets: two theatrical systems
of southern Italy," *Semiotica*, 47(1/4) (1983), pp. 219-280.

[6]In Sicily, as in other parts of Italy, until the 1950's, even the upper classes
used Italian only on formal occasions. The lower middle classes, the peasants, and
the proletariat, spoke dialect almost exclusively. The local language or dialect was
also considered more appropriate for expressing the comic, as was garbled Italian
and pig latin.

[7]Petr Bogatyrev, "The interconnection of two similar semiotic systems: the puppet
theater and living actors," *Semiotica*, 47(1/4) (1983), pp. 47-48.

[8]A similar situation exists in other puppet traditions in which epics are performed,
such as the Liège, Belgium and Indonesia traditions. See papers by Gross and Sherzer
and Sherzer in this volume.

[9]See paper by Sherzer and Sherzer in this volume.

[10]All over the world, comic characters have disproportionate features.

[11]Freud, 1938.

[12]Such differentiation and incongruence, however, is a source of humor in Javanese puppetry. See Alton L. Becker, "Text-building, epistemology, and aesthetics in Javanese shadow theater," in *The imagination of reality*, ed. by Alton L. Becker and Aram Yengoyan (Norwood, New Jersey: Ablex Publishing, 1979), p. 240 and paper by Sherzer and Sherzer in this volume.

[13]Freud, p. 707.

[14]The source used by all puppeteers, the *Storia dei paladini di Francia* by Giusto Lodico, is serious. But Lodico's sources are not. He wrote his prose narrative connecting the plots of a great number of fifteenth and sixteenth century poems, including three classics of Italian literature—Pulci's *Morgante*, Bojardo's *Orlando innamorato*, and Ariosto's *Orlando furioso*—and many other obscure ones, all of which are full of humor. This humor, although altered in tone, has filtered into the *opera dei pupi* through the eighteenth century puppeteers who derived their plots directly from them. In addition, the medieval French epic, the earlier version of the Carolingian legends that was the source of Italian chivalrous literature, was a mixture of comic and serious parts, although its image for the general public is serious. This is due to the fact that the most famous of these *Chansons de Geste*, the *Chanson de Roland*, along with very few others, are serious, and to the prejudices of eighteenth century scholars, who assumed the many *Chansons* which are full of humor are degraded versions of lost, earlier, serious and more noble texts.

In Indonesia, the *punakawan* (Central Java) and *parekan* (Bali), comic characters of the shadow puppet theater, are found only in some of the sources. They are absent, for instance, from the Old Javanese *Ramayana Kekawin* (poem). The first known Javanese literary work which includes clown-servant figures is *Gatotkacasraia* by Panuluh, probably composed in the late twelfth century in east Java. See Th. G. Th. Pigeaud, *Literature of Java* (The Hague: Martinus Njhoff, 1967).

[15]In the *opera dei pupi* and in chivalrous literature the devil is not a representative of evil, but rather an extraordinary instrument of power used either for good or for evil ends by magicians. See Antonio Pasqualino and Janne Vibaek, "Magia rappresentata e magia vissuta, un problema di pertinenza," in *La magia: segno e conflitto* (Palermo: S.F. Flaccovio, 1979), pp. 163-180.

[16]Baudelaire is perhaps the first author who insists on the power of the comic to disrupt tradition. He opposes "ordinary or meaningful comic," employed in the maintenance of social rules and the moral control of behavior, to the grotesque, a more essential, mysterious comic, the "absolute comic." This second type of comic creates a childish dimension, subverts rationality, and opposes the moral of work, sacrifice, and seriousness. Charles Baudelaire, "De l'essence du rire," in *Oeuvres complètes* (Paris: Bibliotèque de la Pléiade, Gallimard, 1961), pp. 710-728; see also "Morale du joujou" (in the same volume) pp. 681-687.

Bergson on the other hand is interested in the repressive function of laughter, that punishes "mechanical degenerations of life." Comic objects appear to be imperfections that oppose the triumph of life produced by modern European society. Henri Bergson, "Le rire, essai sur la signification du comique," in *Oeuvres* (Paris: PUF, 1963 [1900]).

Literary and artistic avant garde movements of the nineteenth century have granted importance to the destructive and aggressive function of laughter and the comic in fighting the crystalized values of bourgeois common sense. (See Ferroni, pp. 98-115). For Bataille laughter is one of the most important weapons to fight ("deconstruct") all possible metaphysical values. But in social life laughter is not always used to destroy; there is a "minor laughter," innocent laughter, used to strengthen cultural values, and a "major laughter" that is the expression of the oppressed, that unvails the weakness of power and kills God and authority. This type of laughter is represented by the festive rituals of reversal. (Georges Bataille, "Le coupable," in *Oeuvres complètes* (Paris: Gallimard, 1973 [1944]; see also Ferroni, pp. 117-143).

For Bakhtin the comic popular tradition is a historic form of laughter, opposing both the seriousness and the comic of power. It can be traced to the Middle Ages and has important literary expressions in the Renaissance. Mikhail Bakhtin, *Rabelais and his World* (Cambridge, Mass.: M.I.T. Press, 1968).

[17]Bergson, p. 22.

[18]"Life" is a central concept in Bergson's philosophy, representing a synthesis of all positive values, a universe of continuous creation, where nothing is repeated. "Mechanism" is the opposite negative concept. Comic objects are mechanical; laughter is the punishment of life's degradation.

[19]Freud writes (p. 797) "everything is comic which does not fit the grown-up" and he adds "I am unable to decide whether the lowering to the level of the child is only a special case of comic degradation or whether everything comical fundamentally depends on the degradation to the level of the child." Baudelaire relates "absolute comic" (as opposed to "ordinary or meaningful comic,") the form of the comic that is useful to society (see note 16), to children's play; both are tendentially destructive. Bergson (who Freud quotes) relates the roots of the comic and of all "émotions joyeuses" to childhood. For Breton, humor, like children's play, connects to "the principle of pleasure," opposing the "principle of reality." (See Ferroni, pp. 21, 22, 39, and 97-98).

[20]Magnin tells of the astonishment of an Italian puppet theater director performing in Paris in 1810 when he found that the audience consisted only of children, whereas in Italy such plays attracted men of all ages. Charles Magnin, *Histoire des marionnettes en Europe depuis l'Antiquité jusqu'à nos jours*, second edition (Paris: M. Lévy Frères, 1862 [1852]) p. 179. Maquet notes that French travelers to Italy, even Stendhal, felt it necessary to introduce the descriptions of puppet plays they had attended with some sort of excuse for giving their attention and attracting the attention of the reader to such a childish subject. Albert Maquet, "Le rire et l'illusion, Stendhal aux marionnettes, à Rome," in *Stendhal, Rome, l'Italie*, ed. by M. Colasanti, A. Tharachimidis, and A.M. Saide (Rome: Edizioni de Storia e Letteratura, 1985), pp. 97-114. By the end of the century, in Italy also puppets were for children.

[21]Magnin, p. 41 and Frank Whiteman Lindsay, *Dramatic parody by marionettes in Eighteenth Century Paris* (New York: King's Crown Press, 1946).

[22]Many common contemporary ideas on puppets can be traced to the second Romanticism, which had a great interest in them and which was instrumental in spreading four distinct ways of conceiving of them (see Daniel Wilhem, *Les romantiques allemands* (Paris: Seuil, 1980), p. 110): 1) The puppet in the hands of the puppeteer is like man in the hands of God or Destiny. (This is a very old idea of puppets, attested in many cultures, for example in the Indian *Bhagavadgita*, in Plato, and in the Arab poets of the twelfth and thirteenth centuries). 2) In creating the puppet man defies God the Creator. The puppet is troublesome (*unheimlisch*), funny, an unhuman thing mimicking man. 3) The puppet is superior to man, an unattainable model for man, because being devoid of conscience it has the perfection and grace of nature that man has lost in creating culture. Henrich von Kleist, *Il teatro delle marionette* (Geneva: il Melangolo, 1978). 4) The puppet theater is an

aspect of "popular culture," conceived as an expression of the collective soul of the Nation and transmits an old and deep wisdom.

[23]Otakar Zich, "Lutkové divadlo [The puppet theater]," *Drobné ûmeni-Vytvarné snahy*, (1923), pp. 4, 7-9, 56-60, and 140-143; and *Estetika dramatického uměni* [*Esthetics of Dramatic Art*] (Prague: Melantrich, 1931).

[24]Bogatyrev, pp. 47-48.

[25]See Henryk Jurkowski, "Transcodification of the sign systems of puppetry," *Semiotica*, 47(1/4) (1983), pp. 123-127.

[26]Giuseppe Pitrè, *Usi costumi, credenze e pregiudizi del popolo siciliano* (Palermo: Pedone Lauriel, 1889).

[27]Jurkowski, pp. 125-127.

[28]Henry Festing Jones, *Diversions in Sicily* (London: A.C. Fifield, 1920).

[29]Think of the desecrating jokes about opera that amuse many fans of this genre. The sensibility of other spectators is sometimes hurt by such jokes, but the possibility of joking about an artistic practice that one loves does not mean that one has a total inability to accept the rules of the system.

[30]Pitrè describes as common episodes of this kind: "when an anecdote, a scene exceeds the limits of the verisimilar or believable, some voices criticize the speaking character and through him the one who speaks for him behind the wings. If the voice from the audience criticizes the historic truth of the tale, the same character, or the comic character of the theater, Nofriu, coming immediately on the scene, retorts to the unwary, exposing him to ridicule." He describes in detail an episode: Orlando had boasted to kill one hundred knights with one blow of his sword. A porter from the audience made a naughty sound and Nofriu retorted: "Read the history if you don't believe it, son of a bitch!" (Pitrè, pp. 129-130).

The Cocreation of the Comic in Puppetry[1]

Frank Proschan

In Plato's allegory of the cave, humans are compared to spectators viewing a puppet show—spectators whose legs and necks are bound to render them immobile.[2] In Euroamerican theater of the last century or so, spectators are immobilized just as completely, but by social conventions rather than binding ropes. Yet contemporary with the elite, literary theater there have existed countless folk and popular theatrical genres and traditions featuring the widest imaginable variety of audience roles and responsibilities. Theorists of the theater have focused so exclusively on the western elite heritage, seeking in its history those elements that persisted rather than those that diverged from the mainstream trends, that little consideration has been given to the active collaboration of audience and artist that characterizes many, if not most, theatrical traditions. In American vaudeville or English music hall, Javanese shadow play or Indian Ramayana performance, magic lantern show or stage magic demonstration, Irish mummers' play or Cherokee booger dance, different expectations for audience behavior prevail and different kinds and degrees of audience participation are encountered.

Every traditional puppetry performance is a collaboration between puppeteer and audience. Each puppetry tradition has its own rules governing the physical relations of stage and audience, the proper forms that spectators' participation should take, the degree to which control of the direction and content of the performance rests with puppeteer or audience members. Yet puppetry characteristically involves collaboration and participation of spectators far more extensive than anything to be found in the modern elite theater. Indeed, the most extreme programmatic pronouncements of avant garde innovators of the last decades demand not the revolution that the theorists intended but instead a return to a relationship of active collaboration like that characteristic of folk theater, and especially folk puppetry.

30

The creative participation of audience members is especially important in the comic genres, or the comic episodes or intervals of more serious performances. World puppetry traditions can be arrayed along a gamut that ranges from the serious domestic tragedies of the Japanese *bunraku* or the puppet stagings of Stravinsky's *Oedipus Rex* to the ribald and hilarious escapades of Punch or Karagioz (or their numerous cousins-in-comedic-crime). The puppetry traditions that tend toward seriousness occasionally approach western art theater in the degree to which spectators are immobilized, passive perceivers. The comic forms of puppetry show us a wide range of roles that the audience can assume during the performance, and demonstrate a number of means and mechanisms by which audience participation is invoked by, shaped for, and incorporated into the performance. It is impossible to understand the comic element in puppetry without investigating how it is cocreated by puppeteer and spectator.

The comedic devices available to the puppeteer are numerous, and not limited to one or another channel. Physical buffoonery and slapstick (the term itself derives from puppetry), humor of situation and circumstance, and verbal humor of many types are characteristic of folk puppetry. Certain kinds of humor predominate in certain traditions. Glove puppets of the family of Punch or Petrushka delight above all in physical byplay, beatings, and virtuoso verbal artistry. The rod marionettes of Sicily are equally violent, although their fights are usually more serious, but humor arises more often from people being in the wrong place at the right time, or from an inherently funny encounter or situation. Occupational, ethnic, and social stereotypes provide a rich resource for humorous portrayal in puppetry.

Language and speech are employed for comic purposes in almost every puppetry tradition. The shadow puppets of Indonesia, for example, take fullest humorous advantage of the multiplicity of functional dialects characteristic of the languages spoken in that country. The satirical or parodistic intent of the authors of European epic texts is often submerged, but an unintended humorous effect sometimes comes from the puppeteer's strivings toward elegant diction. Itinerant puppeteers in multilingual settings have devised comical exchanges that highlight the multiple language skills of their audiences. The foreigner, or the member of an ethnic minority such as Gypsy or Jew, is often at the center of humorous byplay.

Sexuality, bodily functions, and obscenity provide a rich resource for comic exploitation in folk puppetry of many kinds, including even that which originated in sacred observance. The incongruity between or among channels may itself create a comic effect, when a tiny puppet speaks with a deep bass voice while a larger puppet squeaks in contrast, for example. Indeed, the sources of humor in traditional puppetry are as varied as are the traditions as a whole, and as resistant to convenient cataloguing or categorizing.

In what follows I will excavate the foundations upon which all studies of the interaction of puppeteer and audience are based, the work of Petr Bogatyrev and his colleagues in the Prague Circle. I will then turn to an investigation of a single performance by a traditional Punch and Judy professor, Percy Press, Jr., analyzing the dynamics of the performance and the means and mechanisms by which humor is created by performer and spectators working together.

The theoretical explorations of Prague Circle semioticians of the 1930s took place in a milieu where avant-garde experimentation coexisted with nativistic folk revivalism, where intellectuals could recognize and cultivate village traditions at the same time they assaulted classical canons.[3] In such an environment, all expectations and presumptions about aesthetic forms and functions were deautomatized, thrown into question. Petr Bogatyrev, by all accounts an unconventional student of convention, brought to the discussions of the Prague Circle his lifelong fascination with puppetry and folk theater.

The Circle itself, over its dozen years of greatest activity, evokes the image of the Russian fairgrounds in which Bogatyrev conducted his first field researches. Here we have the weightiest philosophical considerations and here the polemics of artist-theorists; there are the case studies and there the abstract theories; now the agendas of language reformers and then the discoveries of linguistic structuralists. Through it all, Bogatyrev wended his way like a Punch man on an English beach or a Petrushka puppeteer in a Moscow park. Indeed, descriptions of him in that era often suggest a resemblance not to a puppeteer but to a puppet character: when invited to a formal dinner at which he was supposed to make a good impression, he took great care to put on a tie, not noticing that he had one tied on already. His lectures and articles were sometimes assembled in the same haste, with friends gathered around at deadline time, pulling his notes together and organizing them into a paper.[4] Whatever they may lack in comprehensiveness or systematicity, his writings nevertheless are pregnant, like Pulcinella's wife, with dozens of prodigal ideas.

Even as early as his first research into folk theater, Bogatyrev was concerned to identify who composed the audience and what their role was in the performance. The fairground traditions that concerned him and his coinvestigator, Roman Jakobson, were not situated in a permanent theater with proscenium and chairs. Rather, spectators milled around a troupe of performers in the open air or in a semi-permanent fairground booth. In either case, the decor was minimal, the staging rudimentary, and the audience transitory. Crucially, the audience was in immediate proximity to the performers, separated not by footlights, stage front, and aisles, but rather by the limits of the booth or by the efforts of a narrator, shill, or money-collector. Moreover, the audience was not bound by the conventions of formal theater, in which viewers are expected to be still and silent, attentive to the goings-on onstage, passive spectators rather than active participants in the stage action. Finally, the composition of the audience could not be assumed in advance, at least not to the same extent that the audience for an elite theatrical performance could be predictably characterized as to class, education, occupation, etc.

For Bogatyrev and Jakobson, then, and for their colleagues later in Prague, the audience's part in theatrical performances was to be discovered, not to be proscribed. Both proceeded from an ethnographic stance, seeking to discover in the exotic certain things that might be obscured in the familiar, at the same time making strange certain commonplace phenomena in order to expose them to more acute scrutiny. The "exotic" traditions could be found not far from the great theaters of Moscow and St. Petersburg, in the fairground booths of Petrushka puppeteers, peep-show expositors, and folk theater troupes. Each of these forms had its own set of rules and roles for its audience, all different from those of the indoor theaters. A questionnaire, developed as a guide for continuing field research in folk theater, returns repeatedly to the composition of the audience and its responsibilities:

Describe as precisely and fully as possible the opinion of different people from the audience about a given play, their thoughts on it, its meanings, and its artistic merits. Give as far as possible information about these people in terms of age, social position, level of education, and so forth.[5]

Even more important, Bogatyrev and Jakobson suggest, are the various ways in which a folk audience participates directly in the performance. They ask, "What part does the public play in the production? Is it only that of an audience or do they intervene in the course of the play: does the audience sing with the chorus, does it answer questions, make retorts, and so forth?."[6]

Intermingled in these questions are two important oppositions that underlay (often in a submerged way) the extensive discussions that ensued within the Prague Circle concerning the audience's participation in theatrical performances. One is the difference between "audience" as a social role subject to social constraints and expectations, and "perceiver" as an individual role governed by psychological functions. The other is the difference between the "intervention" (or, in later Prague terminology, "activation") of the audience or its members in the ongoing performance, and the "cocreation" of meaning and the audience's interpretive work. These distinctions will be useful to keep in mind as heuristic ones, but it must be understood that they were not drawn by Bogatyrev and Jakobson, nor by their later colleagues in Prague. Despite the perspicacity of their research, they never clearly differentiated these concepts (that omission itself, perhaps, testimony to their interrelatedness).

When Bogatyrev moved beyond field research and reportage to interpretation and theorizing, he was influenced most by three thinkers: Otakar Zich, Karl Bühler, and Mikhail Bakhtin. Zich, a Czech aesthetician and critic, discussed two ways in which an audience can perceive puppets: the first was the comic mode in which puppets are perceived "as dolls, that is, we stress their inanimate character.... The result is not, of course, crude comedy but subtle humor which these small figures produce by appearing to act like real people. We perceive them as figurines, but they demand that we take them as people, and this invariably amuses us."[7] In the serious or mysterious mode, the illusion of realness predominates: "our awareness that the puppets are not alive recedes, and we get the feeling of something inexplicable, enigmatic, and astounding.... I think that if our puppets were as large as people, we, too, would feel uneasy, and only their reduced size forestalls this feeling, imparting to them instead a quality of serious mysteriousness."[8]

Bogatyrev's reaction to Zich's article (and his later book on theatrical aesthetics) was colored by his dislike for psychological explanations of social and cultural phenomena. Indeed, his reaction was almost an allergic one, blinding him to the strengths of Zich's arguments at the same time it left the weaknesses uncriticized.[9] Zich's intention was to develop a socially-based psychological theory of perception, as an alternative to aesthetic theories influenced by individualistic or even narcissistic psychologism. Had Bogatyrev recognized the strengths of Zich's approach, he would have found resonances with his own interest in theatrical audiences and their roles and behavior. Instead, he embroiled himself in counterposing examples of puppetry traditions which did not converge neatly with Zich's two trends, in a kind of "ethnographic veto" of the more general arguments that Zich intended. Bogatyrev took special care to establish that "puppet-like" puppets are not necessarily comic and "realistic" puppets are not necessarily serious or mysterious, citing examples from Czech and Russian folk puppetry as well as popular and theatrical forms.[10]

While Zich's aesthetic theories were never explicitly semiotic, Bogatyrev and his Prague colleagues were. His conception of signs and their operations was influenced primarily by two people, Bühler and Bakhtin. Bühler, too, was a psychologist, but like Zich he was interested

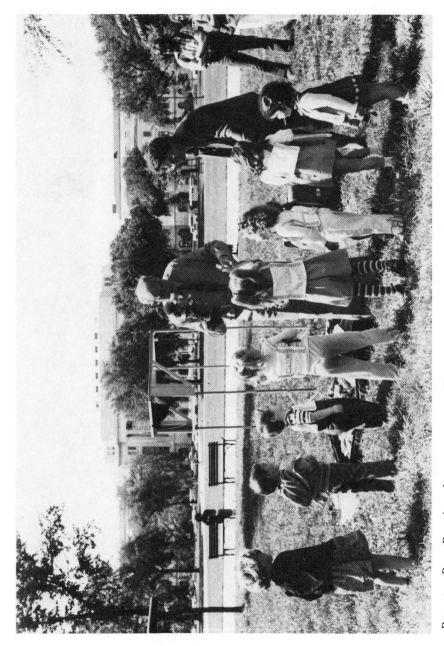

Puppeteer Percy Press introduces puppets to audience.
Photo: C. Kratz

Puppeteer Percy Press talking to audience.
Photo: C. Kratz

Punch and *the Beadle* interacting with the audience.
Photo: C. Kratz

less in individual psychology and more in social psychology. In his classic book on language and sign theory, Bühler identifies three semiotic functions: the *expressive,* inhering in the relation between sign and speaker; the *referential,* inhering in the relation between sign and topic or object; and the *conative,* inhering in the relation between sign and addressee.[11] The conative function, which figured centrally into the Prague scholars' studies of performance audiences, does not involve merely the passive reception of a sign and its meaning, but refers instead to the teleological status of a sign and the perceiver's active apprehension of it.

Finally, Bogatyrev's ideas of semiotics were crystallized by his reading of *Marxism and the Philosophy of Language,* attributed to V.N. Voloshinov but now believed to be the work of Bakhtin.[12] Like Zich and Bühler, Bakhtin was concerned with the social psychology of perception, and he too saw perception not as a passive individual process but as an interactive social one—that is, a process in which meaning is not given but created, and not imposed by the speaker but negotiated together by speaker and hearer. The sociological base of Bogatyrev's semiotic folklore is most apparent in his essays on folk costume,[13] but it is also crucial to his concern with the interaction of performer and audience in traditional theater and puppetry.

The Prague scholars, like their Russian precursors, were also influenced by Saussure's *semiologie,* but they took care not to exaggerate the arbitrary aspect of sign systems. Their emphasis on the social might seem to have led them to view meaning as inherent in the unself-conscious assignments of society, but they rejected the radical Saussurean fissure between synchrony and diachrony, system and history. Whether the sign system is that of folk costume or folk puppetry, the predominant source of meaning is convention—meaning is learned, historically derived, and socially situated, rather than arising mysteriously from unconscious habits located neither in time nor space. It is therefore necessary that one be familiar with a sign system before one can properly understand it, and in many cases necessary that one be taught or even initiated. The naive observer can easily misconstrue the meaning of a complex sign system, especially an artistic one, or construe it in terms of another system, and for Bogatyrev this is the failing of Zich's audiences. The audience members who were frightened by the realistic puppets or amused by the doll-like puppets might merely have been ignorant of the appropriate response, applying the perceptual frame of live theater rather than puppetry.[14]

If one must be properly trained or experienced in order to apprehend and appreciate a performance properly, it is clearly all the more important that one must be initiated into the conventions of audience participation in those performance traditions such as puppetry that depend so heavily upon the active intervention of audience members. In his book on folk theater, Bogatyrev recounts the elaborate intervention of audience members in certain folk plays, as well as spectators' occasional insistence that players perform according to the traditional expectations of the audience.[15] Veltrusky, whose writings in recent years have returned the Prague Circle's conceptions and concerns to the forefront of the semiotics of theater,[16] notes that this degree of interaction is typical—if not definitive—of folk theatrical genres:

> The most developed forms of participation by the spectators can usually be found where the performance is strongly governed by a well-established theatrical convention or where the behavior of the audience is controlled by a close-knit community or both.[17]

Clearly, one characteristic milieu of folk theater and folk puppetry is that where both performer and audience members partake together of a community of interest and a community of expectation. Such a setting, and the genres that flourish within it, provide rich opportunities for humor arising from history and experience—such as, for instance, "in jokes." Topical humor, whether referring to events of the larger civil domain or to personalities of the local realm, often depends on this shared understanding. Yet folk theater forms, and especially folk puppetry, flourish as well in areas of cultural contact and are often performed by itinerant performers.[18] Indeed, sometimes even the language of performance is different from that spoken by the auditors.

In such instances, those conventions specific to a particular group or community may not provide as much of a comic resource as other conventions of more general distribution. For instance, body humor, in which folk puppetry often abounds, or slapstick and buffoonery, refer to what we might be tempted to call universal understandings, rather than local conventions, and we would expect to encounter them frequently in itinerant or multi-cultural performance settings. To be sure, even the most vulgar references are not universal, and Bogatyrev and his colleagues would be among the first to remind us of that simple fact. However, while nothing is funny to everyone, some forms of humor are more likely to amuse more people than other forms are, and we should not be surprised that a puppeteer in a nineteenth century Parisian parlor may delight in slightly risque verbal pleasantries while a Karagioz puppeteer in a working-class tavern provokes laughs with farts and phalluses.

This presentation of the Prague Circle theories has perforce been brief, but sufficient for now to permit us to move on to a consideration of a single puppetry performance that will illustrate how humor is cocreated by performer and spectators, how their collaboration produces the "tragical comedy, or comical tragedy, of Punch and Judy." By examining the various ways by which one traditional Punch professor structures his performance to elicit audience intervention, we see certain techniques that are also utilized by puppeteers from other traditions. Moreover, we see how an uninitiated audience is instructed, without the puppeteer ever overstepping the bounds of the performance frame itself, how to exercise its obligations.

Percy Press Jr.'s performance in Washington, D.C. took place in June, 1980, as part of a series of traditional puppet shows jointly sponsored by the Smithsonian Institution and Puppeteers of America, during the XIIIth World Congress of the international puppeteers' guild, UNIMA. The show was performed on the National Mall, across from the Smithsonian's Museum of History and Technology, to an audience including both those who were there because of an interest in puppetry and those who chanced upon the performance during their touristic rounds. For most, it was doubtless their first authentic Punch and Judy show, and for many, it was their first encounter with a live puppet performance, even if they had been raised on a diet of Sesame Street and other televised puppetry. Certainly few had prior experience as active collaborators in the creation of a puppet performance, or prior initiation into their responsibilities as audience members. Percy Press was faced with the difficult task of involving an untrained, amateur audience in extensive and elaborate participation in the performance. That he succeeded masterfully becomes obvious as we examine excerpts from a transcription of his performance (see the Appendix).

It is useful to delineate four distinct capacities in which the audience members are involved during the show—four roles or identities that they assume. Pasqualino, in a semiotic study of the Italian guaratelle and English Punch, suggests five "methods" used to involve the audience,[19] but here we are more interested in the rhetorical or semantic purposes to which those and other methods can be applied. The four roles that I will discuss are the "Investor," the "Instigator," the "Definer," and the "Ratifier." Assuming each of these identities from time to time, audience members implicate themselves further and further in the action and outcome of the spectacle before them. The general outcome is predictable—although never guaranteed—but the particular details, emphases, and atmosphere of a performance are extremely variable. As we shall see, a successful performance requires that the performer always maintain the upper hand, and that the outcome not diverge too far from what he intends, but a successful performance also requires that the audience seem to have a decisive and determinative role, that its participation be controlled by the puppeteer without seeming to be, and that the whole thing should be fun for both performer and spectator.

The first role, that of "Investor," means that the audience members have some stake in the performance itself. The viewers are implicated and engaged both in the success of the performance itself, as an artistic event, and in the successful conclusion or progression of the enacted events, within the performance frame. I place this first because it was involved especially in the preliminaries to performance. Press brought with him to Washington a portable, folding stage, and he spent as much time unpacking puppets and accessories, assembling the stage, and setting up the performing venue (meanwhile "setting up" the audience itself) as he did in the course of the show's action. By soliciting the physical assistance of children from the crowd, Press created a bustle of activity which in turn attracted other spectators, while ensuring that those already in attendance had some stake in the ensuing performance.

Once the performance began, another technique was used to confirm the audience's engagement: either puppeteer or puppet characters evaluated the communicative competence of the audience members. Press first instructed the audience members in their proper role; they performed it, but were subjected to humorous criticism (Example 1). Thus inspired to do better and participate more forcefully, the children are synchronized into effective partners in the performance. Press clearly establishes for them that the success of the show depends on the audience satisfactorily fulfilling its responsibilities. Later, not just the performance itself but the enacted events were shown to depend on the audience's intervention.

This function merges with the role of "Instigator," where the audience is responsible for instigating actions or for directing events. One or another puppet character repeatedly asks the audience for advice as to a course of action. This is most often done by proposing an action and asking the audience's approval or disapproval. When Punch has his nose bitten by the crocodile, the Doctor arrives and asks the audience what to do (Example 2). Inasmuch as the puppeteer is not prepared to move the action in whatever direction the audience may suggest, he nevertheless creates the impression of being their docile servant. When Doctor Dutch later reveals his true identity as the hangman, Jack Catch, and attempts to hang Punch, the inept executioner refuses to credit the audience's judgment and winds up hanged himself (Example 3).

In its third capacity, the audience is asked not to direct *actions* but instead to direct *interpretations*. This role is that of "Definer" of situations and meanings. This may simply be a matter of naming an object or character (and, when necessary, insisting on its correctness, as in Example

4). More often, however, the audience is asked to report on events that have transpired in the absence of one or another of the puppets—they sum up or distill a complicated set of events. After Punch beats his wife Judy with a slapstick, the audience summons a policeman, to whom they report the beating (Example 5).

In other cases, the audience does not define meanings, but instead acts as "Ratifier" to endorse, corroborate, or contradict meanings or interpretations suggested by one of the puppet characters. For instance, when the Doctor-turned-Hangman is trying to get Punch to put his head into the noose, Punch repeatedly misses, and Jack Catch asks the audience to confirm his (not very complimentary) evaluation of Punch's intelligence (Example 6). Punch's stupidity, confirmed by the audience, in fact turns out to be a ruse, intended to ensnare the all-too-serious executioner.

These examples, severed from the overall story and from the performance context, illustrate various roles that a Punch and Judy audience can be expected to play during the course of the play. The audience's mastery of these roles often contributes to the unfolding of the play's action, moving it along at critical junctures. Yet the audience is also called upon for seemingly inconsequential or gratuitous interventions, whose importance rests in their cumulative incorporation of the audience itself into the performance. Similarly, a repeated refrain with the pattern, "yes you did/no you didn't" encourages all to participate, carried along by the preestablished rhythm of interaction. Crucially, the audience is involved not in a functionary or mechanical capacity, but as cocreators of comedy and pleasure. This comic collaboration takes on added interest when we examine the larger social functions served by the audience's participation in the puppet play.

The audience for Percy Press Jr.'s Washington performance included all ages, but it was especially children between the ages of about five and ten years who were the most vocal participants in the byplay, including that we have just considered. During the performance, they are allowed—indeed, encouraged—to do things that would otherwise be forbidden to them. In Example 1, they are exhorted to express themselves as loudly as possible—certainly not the kind of behavior they are usually encouraged to exercise, especially by a figure of authority. In Example 6, they call someone a stupid idiot, again not normally an acceptable form of expression. These moments of release, fun though they may be, are not nearly as important as some of the other social functions served by this show.

Children of that age range are not normally responsible artistic performers, yet they are implicated directly in the success of the Punch performance. They have a stake in it, to be sure, but they are also held accountable for it. Their "stage directions" are solicited and responded to, and it is not really that important that some of their directions may be declined as Press cleverly channels the children into directing him to do what he intends to do in any case. The puppeteer is not bound by majority rule or who can yell the loudest—from the chorus of sometimes-conflicting voices he can select one to pay attention to, or even wait until he gets just the suggestion that he wants.

The children are not merely asked to provide strategic suggestions or directions, they are also given opportunities to display their cultural competence and expertise. For instance, the scissors/skissors, sausages/swasages interchange in Example 4 allows them to be the cultural experts while contradicting an authority figure. Instead of being faced with teachers or parents who all too often discourage questions (let alone direct contradictions), children in the Punch and Judy audience are given freedom to exhibit superior cultural knowledge. Similarly, by being asked to report on events or to ratify an interpretation of events, children in the audience are given the opportunity to demonstrate their observational skills and to control understandings.

One particular kind of report is often fraught with tension for children—reporting another's infractions (i.e., snitching or tattle-taling). Children are taught that it is proper to be one's sibling's keeper, to be a social conscience, yet when they exercise that function, there is always the possibility for trouble. The situation is tense or unhappy at best, and often the onus of shame or blame is deflected from the wrongdoer onto the reporter. In the Punch show, children can freely indulge their conformist or authoritarian inclinations and can serve as the voice of society, condemning Punch's wife-beating, Joey's sausage-theft, Jack Catch's gullibility, and the repeated lies of one or another character. The puppets can be condemned or contradicted in a spirit of great fun and with little risk of the table being turned.

The children, witnesses together to the events, can speak with one voice, and can speak the truth. By doing so, they create a consensus and shape meaning, and have that meaning accepted by others as the basis for action. In the space of a forty-minute performance, yet with the experience of his own long career, his father's, and those of earlier Punchmen, Percy Press Jr. takes a group of uninitiated and inexperienced spectators, melds them into an audience, teaches them what an audience is supposed to do, and then together they do it. The audience is then held to account for its performance of its assigned duties, and at the same time its opinions, judgments, reports, and interpretations are taken into account by the puppet characters and their manipulator, Professor Percy Press, Jr. Together, they collaborate in the dynamics and the effectiveness of the performance. More importantly, they collaborate in determining what it all means.

Appendix

Examples from a performance of *Punch and Judy* by Percy Press, Jr., Washington, DC, June, 1980.

Example 1

Percy:	...here I come, down the garden path. Good morning, everybody!
Children:	Good morning, Uncle Percy!
Percy:	That was very good, but some of you said "Pussy"—
Children:	(laughter)
Percy:	...—and my name is "Percy." Once more—Good afternoon, everybody!
Children:	Good afternoon, Uncle Percy!
Percy:	Oh, now you all said "Uncle Pussy," but it doesn't matter. I'm going to show you now the 300 years old story of Punch and Judy. Would you like to see Punch and Judy?
Children:	Yes.
Percy:	Oh no you wouldn't!
Children:	Oh yes we would!
Percy:	Oh no you wouldn't! (louder)
Children:	Oh yes we would! (even louder)

Example 2

Doctor Dutch:	What shall I do, then? (with Punch, who has been bitten by a crocodile)
Child A:	Fix him up!
Child B:	Let him die!
Doctor Dutch:	Fix him up? Shall I go downstairs and get him some medicine?
Children:	NO!
Doctor Dutch:	Okay, shall I give him some nasty medicine?
Children:	Yes!
Doctor Dutch:	Okay, down I go for some jolly old nasty medicine—right—girls and boys, I'm downstairs looking for the nasty medicine—I've nearly got it! Girls and boys, shall I bring the nasty medicine up?
Children:	Yes!
Doctor Dutch:	Okay, Punch. Here comes your medicine. Here we come, Punch. Now then, Punch, stand on your feet and take your medicine like a man!
Punch:	That's not medicine!
Doctor:	No, no, Punch, that's not medicine, and I'm not Doctor Dutch either! I am the hangman from England and my name is Jack Catch and I catched you! And what I want you to do, Punch, because you've been so wicked is to

	put your head inside there!
Punch:	Inside there? (missing the noose with his head)
Jack (Doctor):	No, you're stupid! Isn't he stupid, girls and boys?
Children:	Yes!
Jack (Doctor):	I want you, sir, to put your head inside *there*!
Punch:	Inside there? (missing again)
Jack (Doctor):	NO! You're an idiot. Isn't he an idiot, girls and boys? (yelling)
Children:	Yes.
Jack (Doctor):	So! Put your head inside there!
Punch:	Inside there? (missing again)
Jack (Doctor):	NO! In there!
Punch:	Oh, inside here? (missing again)
Jack (Doctor):	NO! Shall I show him myself, boys and girls?
Children:	No—no—no!
Jack (Doctor):	Look, I will show you myself—
Children:	No—
Jack (Doctor):	Look—why, do you think he will trick me?
Children:	Yes!
Jack (Doctor):	Oh no he won't!
Children:	Oh yes he will!
Jerry:	Here they are, everybody. Now tell me, everybody, what do you call these?
Children:	Sausages.
Jerry:	Ah, yes, but I have to call them "swasages," you know why?
Children:	Why?
Jerry:	Because I cannot say "sausages."
Children:	You just said it!
Jerry:	No! I said "swasages." I can't say "sausages."
Children:	You just said it again!
Jerry:	And another thing, everybody, I have to say "skissors" because I can't say "scissors." But anyway—
Children:	You just said "scissors."
Judy:	Girls and boys, call the policeman! Call the policeman, call the policeman—
Children:	Police! Police!
Policeman:	(humming) Right, that's me, here I come, I've got a bit stuck here—Hello, everybody!
Children:	Hello!
Policeman:	I am the policeman from England. Tell me, what is the trouble?
Children:	He's hitting her— He's hitting his wife and baby with the stick—
Policeman:	Punch hit his wife with a stick?
Children:	Yes, and the baby!
Policeman:	And the baby?

Example 6

Example 3

Example 4

ample 5

	Children:	Yes!
	Punch:	Oh no I never!
Ex	Children:	Oh yes you did!

Notes

[1]An earlier version of this paper was presented at the 1984 meetings of the American Anthropological Association. Its preparation was supported by the University of Texas at Austin and the Smithsonian Institution. Percy Press Jr.'s performance was sponsored by the Smithsonian Institution and Puppeteers of America; it was videotaped by the University of Texas with funding from the National Endowment for the Humanities. Bill Gradante assisted with the transcription.

[2]Plato, *The Republic*, 514.

[3]See, for example, Roman Jakobson, "Petr Bogatyrev (29.I.93—18.VIII.71): Expert in transfiguration," in *Sound, Sign, and Meaning*, ed. by Ladislav Matejka (Ann Arbor: University of Michigan, 1976), pp. 29-39; Roman Jakobson and Krystyna Pomorska, *Dialogues* (Cambridge: MIT Press, 1983); *Change* 3 (1969) and 10 (1972).

[4]Svatava Pirkova Jakobson, personal communications.

[5]Petr Bogatyrev, *Cesski Kukol'nyj i russkij narodnyj teatr* (Berlin-Petersburg: Opojaz, 1923), p. 106.

[6]Bogatyrev, p. 103.

[7]Otakar Zich, "Loutkove divadlo," *Drobne umeni—vytvarne snahy* 4 (1923), p. 8.

[8]Zich, p. 9.

[9]See Jiri Veltrusky, "Puppetry and acting," *Semiotica* 47 (1983), 109.

[10]Petr Bogatyrev, *Lidove divadlo ceske a slovenske* (Prague: Borovy, 1940); "A contribution to the study of theatrical signs," in *The Prague school: selected writings 1929-1946*, ed, by Peter Steiner (Austin: University of Texas Press, 1982), pp. 55-64 [first published 1937-1938]; "The interconnection of two similar semiotic systems: the puppet theater and the theater of living actors," *Semiotica*, 47 (1983), pp. 47-68 [first published 1973].

[11]Karl Buhler, *Sprachtheorie* (Jena: G. Fischer, 1934); see also Roman Jakobson, "Concluding statement: linguistics and poetics," in *Style in Language*, ed. by Thomas A. Sebeok (Cambridge: MIT Press, 1960), pp. 350-377.

[12]V.N. Voloshinov, *Marxism and the philosophy of language* (Cambridge: Harvard University Press, 1986) [first published 1929].

[13]Petr Bogatyrev, "Costume as a sign," in *Semiotics of art: Prague school contributions*, ed. by Ladislav Matejka and Irwin R. Titunik (Cambridge: MIT Press, 1976), pp. 13-19 [first published 1936]; *The functions of folk costume in Moravian Slovakia* (The Hague: Mouton, 1971) [first published 1937].

[14]Bogatyrev, "The interconnection . . ." p. 49.

[15]Bogatyrev, *Lidove divadlo . . .*

[16]Jiri Veltrusky, "Contribution to the semiotics of acting," in *Sound, sign, meaning*, ed. by Ladislav Matejka, (Ann Arbor: University of Michigan Press), pp. 553-606; "The Prague school theory of theater," *Poetics Today*, 2 (1981), pp. 225-235; "Puppetry and acting."

[17]Veltrusky, "Contribution . . .," p. 592.

[18]Frank Proschan, "Puppet voices and interlocutors: language in folk puppetry," *Journal of American Folklore*, 94 (1981), pp. 527-555.

[19]Antonio Pasqualino, "Marionettes and glove puppets: two theatrical systems of Southern Italy," *Semiotica*, 47 (1983), pp. 219-280.

Verbal Humor
in
The Puppet Theater

Dina and Joel Sherzer

Puppetry is an expressive and artistic form which is extremely widespread in the world, is ancient and traditional in many cultures, and is developing and innovating everywhere it is found. Yet despite its omnipresence, despite its visual, linguistic, artistic, social, cultural, and historical significance, it has until recently received relatively little scholarly attention.[1] And that aspect of puppetry which is of concern here, verbal humor, has received the least. This scholarly lack of attention may be because of the usual setting of puppetry, the social and physical location of its occurrence—originally in fairs, markets, and carnivals, the gathering place of the lower and popular classes, and, more recently, especially in the West, in museums, schools, and libraries, where it is intended for children and, unfortunately, has lost much of its satirical bite. Furthermore, the language of puppetry is based on various forms of speech play, including puns and verbal dueling, which are deemed unimportant and secondary by most scholars of high culture.[2] In a few places, most notably Indonesia, where puppetry is associated with and performed for ritual and ceremonial occasions, it is not considered to be a lowly genre and has accordingly received scholarly attention.[3]

Of the various intersecting semiotic systems in puppetry (language, gestures, colors, clothing, sets, stages, etc.), the focus here is on the verbal, and, in particular, on verbal humor, on the nature of humorous language and speech. The discussion consists of two parts: first how is verbal humor created in the different puppetry traditions and second what is the significance and function of this verbal humor.

These remarks are based on extensive personal observation of a wide variety of puppet traditions—Indonesian shadow, glove, and human puppets; Japanese Bunraku; Indian marionette and shadow puppets; Egyptian Aragoz and the related Turkish Karagoz; Sicilian *pupi*, Belgian and northern French marionettes; British Punch and Judy; and the

Brazilian Mamulengo—as well as a survey of the existing literature. The contribution of this paper is to bring to bear on puppetry a modern sociolinguistic and discourse analytic perspective together with a cross-cultural and comparative approach. While the focus is traditional puppetry, modern puppetry shares some of the features discussed as well. And given the improvisational and innovative nature of traditional puppetry, it is sometimes difficult to draw the line between traditional and modern puppetry.

There are certain features of the role and use of language in puppetry which are inherently comical. These are overarching features which cut across traditions, genres, and puppet types. What is a puppet? Typically, it is a small, inanimate object, made of wood, metal, leather, straw, or rags, and capable of speaking, that is, it is a nonhuman object gifted with the most human of abilities, that of speech. By speech is understood a complex system of communication which involves conversations and interactions using a variety of voices. Furthermore, it is the speech of adults as well as that of children which emanates from these figures generally the size of dolls. During a puppet performance quite diverse and disproportionate elements are combined—animate and inanimate, human and object, large and small, and adult and child. This very nature of the puppet, its very semiotic constitution, is a source of humor in the basic sense in which Freud defines it, that is, as an unexpected and incongruous juxtaposition of quite distinct entities. And language is central to this.

But it is not only because inanimate objects talk during puppet performances that they are humorous. There is in particular the special nature of the production of voices in puppet drama, the fact that it is usually a single individual who creates a wide variety of voices.[4] This single individual is capable of imitating the sociolinguistic repertoire of an entire society, community, or region, and even beyond. A puppeteer imitates not only dialects and styles of speaker, but also accents of all kinds, including the voices associated with physical and personality types, gender, and age, as well as speech defects.[5] Noises of many types also emanate from these puppet mouths and other orifices of their little bodies—shouts, screams, whistles, cries, whispers, weeps, laughs, nose blows, snores, yawns, coughs, sneezes, groans, grunts, burps, and farts. One of the most impressive voice producers is clearly the Indonesian *dalang* who distinguishes forty to sixty characters in performance. The Turkish Karagöz theater traditionally had fifty to sixty figures, all with distinct ways of speaking.[6] The variety of voices heard at a puppet show typically involves a much wider range than playgoers are likely to hear in a live theater with a full cast of real human actors. This one man/

many puppet show is humorous because of the exaggeration and accumulation of voices and noises.

In this display of voices, often involving rapid movement from language to language, dialect to dialect, style to style, and accent to accent, many features and possibilities of the vocal apparatus are employed, including tempo, loudness, pitch, musicality, and types of pronunciation, as well as syntax, semantics, and vocabulary. Modifications of the voice, such as nasality and hoarseness, are common and the use of a physical voice modifier inserted into the mouth is widespread.[7]

These juxtapositions of languages, dialects, styles, and accents have comic effects, again, because of the disjunctions produced by the copresence of upper and lower class, formal and informal, polite and rude, stilted and popular, and esoteric and vulgar speech, along with the social, cultural, and historical connotations of these sociolinguistic levels. It has been noted that

It is not the gestures, the individual behaviour, and the characteristic clothes that have enabled them [puppets] to live through the centuries. Admittedly, these have exerted some influence, but their immortality lies in their speech and accent; their inspired use of those rich dialects and patois which have their very roots in the souls of the people, and possess a rare appeal as sound alone, while the slurred words and clipped sentences have a myriad shades of meaning, the full value of which can be appreciated only by those who have spent their lives in the districts concerned.[8]

Examples abound.[9] The Bunraku plays written by the famous Japanese author of puppet plays Chikamatsu distinguish thirteen different levels of politeness for the female characters alone. The Indonesian *dalang* uses Sanskrit, Old Javanese, Indonesian, colloquial Javanese and Balinese (and many levels of politeness within them), and even Dutch, French, English and Japanese. The itinerant South Indian puppets from Karnataka use several Dravidian and Indo-Aryan languages. The shadow puppets of the Turkish Karagoz theater speak with all of the accents of the Ottoman empire—Albanian, Armenian, Greek, Kurd, Persian, Arabic, Gypsy, Jewish, etc. Brazilian Mamulengo puppets mingle the Portuguese accent of the Northeast with that of the large cities of the South, Sao Paulo and Rio de Janeiro. The puppets in the Belgian tradition of Liège speak the local language Walloon, as well as various dialects and styles of French. Similarly the Guignol puppets of Lyon speak the local Lyon dialect as well as French and the puppets of the northern French city of Amiens speak both Picard and French. Sicilian *pupi* speak both Italian and Sicilian and various dialects of each. Papa Manteo's New York City version of the Sicilian *pupi* adds English to this repertoire.

Contemporary audiences find the constant shifting among Italian, Sicilian, and English quite humorous. Here are some examples from one of their performances.[10] The speaker is Fiordiligi, the major heroine.

Mio caro Ricardo. Como sono felice. You're in love with me and I'm in love with you.
Please please o o allontanati allontanati. Don't stay near me. Don't touch me. Please. I hate you.
Oh I will never forget him. Non dimentichero mai il paladino Rolando.

A puppet show is a veritable microcosmic reframing[11] of the sociolinguistic structure of a speech community. The juxtaposition of many languages, dialects, styles, accents, and noises is not only a comical device in and of itself. It serves as well as a resource for creating further comical effects, those of stereotype and exaggeration. For a single individual (the puppeteer) to create the wide variety of voices used in a puppet performance involves an extreme exaggeration of their distinctive traits, that is, these many voices are all created by means of stereotype, caricature, impersonation, mimicry, parody, and mockery of actual language use. This distortion and manipulation of the sociolinguistic system of a community can have quite humorous results.

Sometimes the exaggeration and stereotyping of voices is quite systematic. The Indonesian case is particularly structured and refined.

The *dalang* learns to reshape his mouth and alter his entire vocal mechanism systematically to distinguish certain characters and types of characters. Pushing the points of the articulation of sounds forward in the mouth suggests refinement and culture, pushing them back toward the throat suggests roughness and raw nature.... Steady, even pitch and rhythm suggest impulsiveness, a dimension of character very important to Javanese.[12]

Voice quality is also related to body size. "Larger figures have lower and more resonant voices, while the voices of smaller figures are higher pitched and, more noticeable, are thinner in quality."[13]

A different utilization of the voice stereotypes social rank in the Liège puppetry of Belgium.

Subordinate characters have higher pitch, softer intensity, and little variation in both, while the opposite is found in the voices of dominant characters. A voice qualification that is indicative of subordination—or more specifically cowardliness in battle—is stuttering.[14]

These cases of stereotype and caricature involve a systematic pattern for an entire speech community or social ranking system. There are also many instances of particular, individual impersonations and parodies.

The Greek and Turkish Karagoz theaters provide hilarious stereotypes of the many accents one encounters in the multiethnic and multilingual meeting places of Europe and Asia. Here is a description of the renowned Athens' puppeteer Anton Mollas.

Mollas speaks all the dialogue. And this is quite a task for each personage has his or her distinctive voice; and there can be no mistaking them when they are off-stage. There is the rich dignified voice of the Vizier; Barba-George's gruff, peasant voice; the honied, hypocritical tones of Khatziavatis; the sing-song, monotonous voice of Nionios the Zantiote; the heady voice of the Jews; and the subtly different Greek accents of the different islanders. The voice of Karagoz himself is a strident yet amazingly varied baritone that can rise to a mirth-provoking falsetto or descend to a frightening basso-profundo.[15]

Contemporary Turkish Karagoz performances mock the accents of returning Turkish guest workers from Germany.

Punch and Judy shows traditionally include a Black puppet who speaks in a stereotyped Black accent. Here is an example of Percy Press' Black singing a Calypso-like song with a stereotyped Caribbean accent.[16]

Somebody bad stole de wedding bell.
Somebody bad stole de wedding bell.
Somebody bad stole de wedding bell.
Somebody bad stole de wedding bell.

The discussion so far has dealt in general terms with the devices which create the verbal humor of puppetry. But puppetry is a quite variable form of expression. It proves useful to group puppet performances into two types—enactments of stories, often long epics, and short, focused farces. This typology cuts across the usual typology of the physical nature of puppets into shadow, rod/string, and hand/glove puppets, although it might be argued that hand/glove puppets lend themselves to farces and not to epics.

A good example of a performance of an epic comes from Indian and Indonesian puppetry. The ancient Indic epics, the *Ramayana* and the *Mahabarata*, which are enacted in these traditions, can last all night long. Epics were also performed in Europe, most notably in the Liège, Belgium and the Sicilian traditions. The Charlemagne epics which are performed by Sicilian *pupi* were stretched out into many episodes in soap opera-like fashion over long periods of time. In both Sicily and in New York City, the full performance of an epic lasted an entire year or longer, during which audiences followed the story night after night.

There are several sources of verbal humor within epic performances, which clearly also involve narrative elements not intended to be comical. The puppet enactments are a reframing, in a comical key[17] of chivalric epics which for centuries have been performed in many forms, including the narrative speaking and chanting of troubadour-like individuals, in which the taking on and imitation of voices was prominent.[18] The Ariosto version of the Charlemagne epics, used as a source by the Sicilian puppeteers, and the *Bibliothèque bleue* versions, employed by the Belgians, are already comic because they themselves are reframed parodies of serious texts. The South Indian Karnataka shadow puppets enact a quite clearly popular version of the classical Indian *Ramayana* epic. The performance is most lively, including an exuberant, exaggerated use of music, gesturing, fighting, and dancing. Women in particular are less controlled and more boisterous in their behavior than the "ideal," "refined" classical model would probably portray them.

The stereotyping and exaggeration of sociolinguistic distinctions, which we described above as a feature common to all puppetry, is another comical element of the enactment of epics. In Indonesia, in which the sociolinguistic structure of all speech, human and puppet, is most complicated, a particularly refined type of humor occurs in epic performances, involving a purposeful incongruity between voices on the one hand and associated eye shapes, head angles, ornamentations and clothing, stances, and arm and body movements on the other.[19]

Still another comical element within epic performances is the use of various types of comical figures. Belgian enactments of the Charlemagne epics include as an actor Tchantchès, a contemporary Liège worker whose humor derives from his temporal and social incongruity within these medieval epics, as well as his trickster-like verbal behavior. He is also a metalinguistic commentator on the action, using Walloon, the popular working class dialect/language of French-speaking Belgium. The Indonesian clownish figures, even more obviously, constitute comic figures within a more serious drama. While their official role is to translate the ancient languages spoken by nobles and Gods into the modern languages of contemporary Indonesia, these figures, like their Sicilian *pupi* counterparts, the comical Nofriu, Virticchiu, and Peppeninu, often perform comical interludes between acts or episodes of epic dramas. These interludes are farces within the epics and for this reason we can now turn directly to an examination of farces.

Farces, whether they constitute the entirety of a puppet performance, such as the French Guignol, the Italian Pulcinella, the Egyptian, Turkish, Greek Aragoz/Karagoz, or the British Punch and Judy, or are comical interludes within longer dramas, such as the Indonesian and Sicilian epics, are always characterized by an exploration of and indeed celebration of the total gamut of forms of speech play and verbal humor. These include puns, riddles, proverbs, nonsense, scatological language, endless repetitions, verbal repartee and dueling, grammatical deviations, interactional manipulations, breaking of social norms, and satire. Playing with frames of interpretation and performance and trickster behavior are always paramount. Every aspect of language, from sounds to sociolinguistic patterns, is affected. A typology of examples illustrates their complex and rich diversity.

The clown-like characters who perform farces as interludes within epic dramas are exuberant sociolinguistic tricksters. In particular, they make fun of upper caste and class dialects, no doubt to the delight of popular and lower class audiences. Indonesian clownish figures alternate between colloquial contemporary languages such as Javanese and Balinese, in which they improvise satirical, biting commentary, and Old Javanese or Sanskrit, ancient languages unintelligible to their audiences. What could be funnier than a lower class, popular character, burping and farting, and at the same time speaking the most elegant of old Javanese or Sanskrit, thus mocking both these languages themselves and the arbitrariness of the caste and religious structure they reflect. Italian comic characters speak Sicilian dialect and occasionally an intentionally garbled Italian.

Certain personages of a higher social order, such as judges and doctors, make frequent use of Italian expressions, often garbled on purpose to add humorous and negative values. The priest is often caricatured by making him speak pig-latin.[20]

All farces include parodies of speech styles and accents. The accents of foreigners are particularly mocked. Examples include mocking of the French invaders of Sicily speaking Italian, by Sicilian *pupi*, of returning guest workers speaking Turkish with a German accent, by Karagoz, and of tourist and salespersons speaking Portuguese, by Brazilian mamulengo. Here is an imitation of a Swiss French accent from an eighteenth century French Polichinelle show, in which the "mistakes" in French result in puns and word play such as *foutriez-fous* "screw-crazy" for *voudriez-vous* "would you please" and *poire de fin* "pear of end" for *boire de vin* "drink wine", the first case creates a sexual innuendo, the second, garbled French.

LE SWISSE

Parti, par mon foy, montsir Poliquinelle,
Foutriez-fous pien tans sti jour
Me donné'rien p'tit leçon t'amour
Et sur le charcon de sti cour?

Malay shadow puppets
Two serious characters and two clowns
Photo: A. Pasqualino

Punch and Judy.
Photo: A. Pasqualino

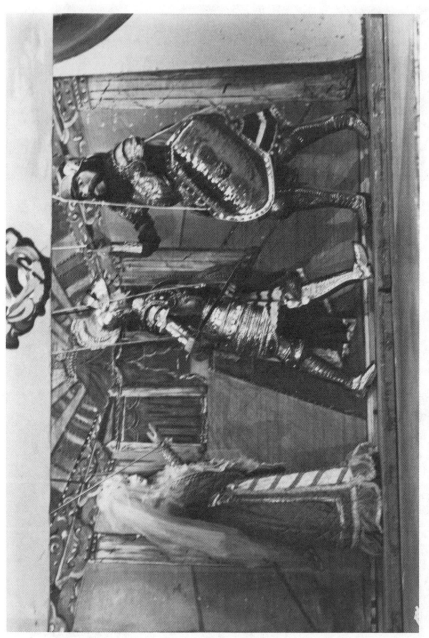

Papa Manteo's New York City *Pupi*: Fiordiligi, Ricardo, and Balahin

Photo: C. Kratz

Javanese *wayang kulit purwa* contrasts the righteous (l.) Pandawa brothers with their treacherous cousins, the Kurawa (r.) The *kayon* (tree of life) sits in the middle of the screen showing that this is the end of the performance.
Photo: K. Foley

POLICHINELLE
Mais, montsir, si vous ne vous taisez, vous serez
quatre jours sans boire de vin.

LE SWISSE
Quatre jours sans poire de fin![21]

Word play of all kinds, including puns, abounds. Here are some
French examples: From the puppet tradition of the northern French city
of Lille, a hypercorrection stemming from the local dialect causes
"Lohengrin" to become "l'iau(water) en grain."[22] Also from the Lille
tradition, a classic spoonerism: "Monsieur le baron, madame la baronne
est venue molle à la fesse!" ("Monsieur the baron, madame the baronesse
became soft in the buttocks") in which *molle à la fesse* "soft in the
buttocks" is a transformation of *folle à la messe* "crazy at mass."[23] Here
is a classic pun from Punch and Judy which occurs when the puppeteer
is introducing a new character: "This everyone is Dr. Duck. He's a bit
of a quack."[24] The Punch and Judy show also incongruously accumulates
and associates words and expressions by means of repetition with
variation. Here is the puppeteer speaking to the audience: "Good
morning. Good afternoon. Good night. Good gracious. Good Friday.
Whitmonday," And Punch's voice-distorting voice modifier enables him
to produce quite far-fetched phonic effects, as in this classic series in
which Punch is talking to Jack Ketch, the Hangman:[25]

JACK: Punch, put your head in the—like this—in the loop.
PUNCH: In the soup.
JACK: Not in the soup.
CHILD (in audience): In the loop.
JACK: That's right. In the loop.
PUNCH: Soup.
JACK: Not soup. And I want you to say "Ladies and gentlemen, I have been a
wicked man."
PUNCH: I want some bread and jam.
JACK: Not you "want some bread and jam.:" "I've been a wicked man and the
law has found me guilty."
PUNCH: And the floor is jolly dirty.
JACK: Not "the floor is jolly dirty." "The law has found me guilty and I must
hang by the neck until I am dead, dead, dead."
PUNCH: Bread, bread, bread.

The Balinese shadow puppet theater is literally teeming with puns,
repetitions of words and phrases, jokes, riddles, and manipulated
proverbs. The resulting language is off-color, bordering on the obscene,

and always outrageously, irreverently, and shamelessly disrespectful. The audience loves it all.

All of these examples display a veritable exploration and exploitation of the similarities and differences that exist in various aspects of language.

Like Groucho Marx, as well as some avant garde, experimental theater, puppet farces include much breaking of frame and interacting with the audience, often tricking participants within it. The Liège, Belgium trickster-hero Tchantchès returns to the stage during intermission "often asking the children in the audience to help him 'bury' the dead soldiers and knights who died during the battles and whose wooden bodies must be cleared from the stage."[26] In the Italian Pulcinella show, the following methods are employed to involve the audience:

(1) a puppet asks the audience to help him by alerting him whenever a certain character appears, either so that he can attack him or in order to warn him of a potential aggression on that character's part;

(2) a puppet asks the audience to help him by giving him information about what happened on stage in his absence;

(3) a puppet asks the audience to help him by giving advice on whether or not to carry out an action;

(4) a puppet, the puppeteer, or the outside intermediary asks the audience to exchange greetings with him;

(5) a puppet, the puppeteer, or the outside intermediary asks the audience to confirm the name of a character or an object.[27]

The British Punch and Judy displays these same features. Here is the puppeteer opening his show.[28]

PUPPETEER: Would you like to see Punch and Judy?
AUDIENCE: Yes.
PUPPETEER: Oh no you wouldn't.
AUDIENCE: Yes we would.
PUPPETEER: Oh no you wouldn't.
AUDIENCE: Oh yes we would.
PUPPETEER: OK I'll go to the back.

Here a puppet actor interprets Punch's distorted voice for the audience:

JUDY: Punch?
PUNCH: Yes.
JUDY: What do you want?
PUNCH: A kiss.
JUDY: A kiss. Boys and girls, should I give Punch a kiss?

Here a puppet actor, the policeman, invites a member of the audience to join in the performance, using the opportunity to improvise a pun on her name: ,

POLICEMAN: What is your name?
CHILD: Justin.
POLICEMAN: Justin. Look Justin. If you call for me next time, we'll be just in time to catch him.

Finally, here another puppet, Joey the clown, tricks the audience and in so doing offers a subtle commentary on the arbitrariness of correct pronunciation, in a classic Punch and Judy routine:

JOEY: Now tell me everybody what do you call these?
AUDIENCE: Sausages.
JOEY: Ah yes. But I have to call them swasages, you know why?
AUDIENCE: Why?
JOEY: Because I cannot say sausages.
AUDIENCE: You just said it.
Joey: No, I said swasages I can't say sausages.

Frame breaking is a form of metacommunication. Another is commentary on words or actions as or after they occur, also a common feature of puppetry. The clown-like characters in the Balinese shadow puppet theater often comment metacommunicatively on each other's breaking of the rules of sociolinguistic etiquette. Here is a typical exchange between Tualen and Wredah, two translator-clowns.[29]

TUALEN: Baladéwa nyebak.
          Baladéwa is bawling.
WREDAH: Da kétoanga ibané ngomong.
          Don't speak like that.

Tualen's line is funny because he uses the word nyebak for "crying."
There are three words for crying in Balinese.

(1) menangis is the high form, appropriate to deities and nobles such as Baladéwa and should have been used here.
(2) ngeling is the middle form, used for lower caste, ordinary individuals: this form would have been inappropriate here.
(3) nyebak is the low form, used in order to be purposefully disrespectful and insulting. We have thus translated it as bawling. It is irreverently and outrageously out of place here.

Wredah's response is a metacommunicative scolding of Tualen's sociolinguistic blunder. In what follows these puppets go on to complain about the way people no longer use appropriate language for nobles. Such metacommunicative commentary and discussion of the language of social caste and class, quite common within the Balinese puppet theater, is both a satirical and almost subversive attack on ancient, rigid, and ritual sociolinguistic rules and a humorous reflection of and on a rapidly and radically changing social and linguistic situation within modern, contemporary Indonesia.

What is the significance of verbal humor in the puppet theater? Seemingly small and insignificant, puppets are by no means trivial. They are the locus of an intersection of speech play and verbal art of all kinds. They incorporate high, popular, and folk art, seriousness and humor, culture and politics, adults and children. They are a complex and polyvalent expressive form in which the verbal and the visual resources and possibilities offered by society, culture, politics, and history are exploited to the fullest. They are definitely worth preserving and worth studying.

The fact of putting words into another's mouth, especially the mouth of an inanimate object and in a language, dialect, style, or accent distanced from one's own, seems to make puppetry a particularly appropriate form for social and political satire, especially in situations in which other means are not permissible. Satire typically involves improvisation. Itinerant Indonesian *dalangs* learn of local happenings and their shadow clowns improvise often allusive satirical skits in the regional languages and dialects, criticizing local businessmen and officials, as well as corruption in the national government. The South Indian Karnataka performers are paid by local supporters to attack verbally certain individuals.

Socially critical satire is particularly prominent in farces. The scatological language of Guignol in Lyon, France was so politically satirical during the Second Empire that the government banned performances. Nineteenth century missionaries tried to put an end to the satirical traditional Hawaiian puppetry and contributed to its eventual demise. The Karagoz theater was continuously persecuted by the sultans of the Turkish Empire. Ironically, it is said that in Cairo only Aragoz could insult the sultan.

As has been shown here, puppets express and indeed celebrate the vitality of language and speech. They clearly demonstrate that language should not be viewed as a static or frozen system, but rather as a dynamic one, available for play, manipulation, and creativity at every level— phonic, grammatical, semantic, and sociolinguistic. Puppets share this approach to language with Rabelais, Lewis Carroll, Groucho Marx,

Eugene Ionesco, Samuel Beckett, and young children, all of whom treat language in creative ways often alien to adults.[30] In their full exploitation of the sociolinguistic resources of language, puppets provide a counterpoint to high culture, highlighting modes of popular culture, especially popular verbal culture, often considered inferior by the dominant sterilizing, homogenizing, and standardizing social structure. Against the backdrop of the static, sterile, and standardizing approach to language of the dominant social classes, puppets celebrate diversity, earthiness, vitality, difference, exuberance, and spontaneity.

As comical as they are then puppets are involved in quite serious business. They juxtapose fantasy and reality and as such can be quite humorous. But the reality they represent is the concrete world of social actors with real voices, ultimately the entire set of voices of a community. What is the serious function of a comic form based on the sociolinguistic situation of a community or a region? Like all humor, the humor of puppets is a subversive one. It makes fun of the linguistic differences which reflect purely arbitrary and conventional social differences. But it also attracts attention, in a most positive way, to linguistic diversity, play, and creativity, and so doing highlights and positively values this diversity, play, and creativity. At the same time and again like many if not all forms of comedy and humor, puppets offer an alternative to the serious world we live in and when satirical and socially and politically critical provide a carnivalesque letting off of steam.

Puppets are also relevant to linguistic issues, and especially to sociolinguistics, because of insights they provide concerning relationships among language, culture, society, and the individual. They reflect native perceptions and conceptions of sociolinguistic distinctions and show how native members of communities manipulate and play with these distinctions. They point to areas of language in which play and manipulation are possible and indeed occur. They focus in a most interesting way on the interplay of the individual and society in language use in that one person mimics the whole speech community. And they reveal an exuberant set of playful forms of discourse in use in communities, the puns, jokes, riddles and verbal tricks that have often persisted for generations.

It is interesting that in spite of the geographic, cultural, and linguistic diversity there are remarkable similarities in the form and the function of puppets and in the ways in which they play with and manipulate language. In puppets from societies as different as Rajastan and modern London, Bali and Rio de Janeiro, these forms of play, humor, and biting social relevance are being created and recreated, mingling the serious and the comic, the grotesque and the grave, and the trivial and the refined.[31]

Notes

[1]Notable examples of scholarly, book-length treatments of puppetry are James R. Brandon, ed., *On Thrones of Gold: Three Javanese Shadow Plays* (Cambridge: Harvard University Press, 1970); Paul Fournel, ed., *Les Marionnettes* (Paris: Bordas, 1982); Ward Keeler, *Javanese Shadow Plays* (Princeton: Princeton University Press, 1987); Donald Keene, *Bunraku. The Art of the Japanese Puppet Theater* (Tokyo: Kodansha International Ltd., 1965); Roger Long, *Javanese Shadow Theatre: Movement and Characterization in Ngayogyakarta Wayang Kulit* (Ann Arbor; UMI Research Press, 1982); Katharine Luomala, *Hula Ki'i: Hawaiian Puppetry* (Honolulu: Institute for Polynesian Studies, 1984); Michael R. Malkin, *Traditional and Folk Puppets of the World* (New York: A.S. Barnes and Co., 1977); Antonio Pasqualino, *L'Opera dei Pupi* (Palermo: Sellerio editore, 1977); Frank Proschan, ed., *Puppets, Masks and Performing Objects from Semiotic Perspectives (Semiotica* 47(1/4), 1983); George Speaight, *The History of the English Puppet Theater* (New York: John de Graff, 1955); and Mary Zurbuchen, *The Shadow Theater of Bali: Explorations in language and text.* (Princeton: Princeton University Press, 1987).

[2]See Barbara Kirshenblatt-Gimblett, ed., *Speech Play* (Philadelphia: University of Pennsylvania Press, 1976) for the significance of speech play in general.

[3]See Alton L. Becker, "Text-building, epistemology, and aesthetics in Javanese Shadow Theater," in *The Imagination of Reality*, ed. by Alton L. Becker and Aram Yengoyan (Norwood, New Jersey: Ablex Publishing, 1979), pp. 211-243; Annie Bernard, "Les Marionnettes Indonésiennes," in *Les Marionnettes*, ed. by Paul Fournel (Paris: Bordas, 1982), pp. 63-67; Olive Blackham, *Shadow Puppets* (London: Barrie and Rockliff, 1960); Brandon, p. 25; Hedi Hinzler, *Bima Swarga in Balinese Wayang* (Verhandelingen van het Koninklijk Instituut voor Taal-,Land-en Volkenkunde 90) (The Hague: Martinus Nijhoff, 1981); Keeler; Long; Colin McPhee, "The Balinese Wayang Kulit and its Music," *Djawa* 16 (1936) pp. 1-34; Jeune Scott-Kemball, *Javanese Shadow Puppets* (Great Britain: Shenval Press, 1970); Amin Sweeney, *The Ramayana and the Malay Shadow Play* (Kuala Lumpur: National University of Malaysia Press, 1972); and H. Ulbricht, *Wayang Purwa: Shadows of the Past* (Kuala Lumpur: Oxford University Press, 1970); and Zurbuchen.

[4]Among the puppet performances we have observed, the Punch and Judy, the Liège rod puppet, and the Turkish Karagoz puppeteers each alone created all of the voices, men as well as women. Papa Manteo, of the New York Sicilian marionettes, creates all the male voices while his sister Ida creates the female voices.

[5]It is worth noting that the dramatization of voices is a widespread characteristic of oral narratives, especially those performed in nonliterate societies. For an American Indian tradition, see Edward Sapir, *Abnormal Types of Speech in Nootka* (Canada, Department of Mines, Geological Survey, Memoir 62, Anthropological Series, 5, 1915).

[6]See Brandon, p. 62 and René Simmen, *The World of Puppets* (New York: Thomas Y. Crowell, 1972), p. 96.

[7]On voice modifiers, see Frank Proschan, "Puppet Voices and Interlocutors: Language in Folk Puppetry," *Journal of American Folklore*, 94 (1981), pp. 527-555.

[8]Cyril Beaumont, *Puppets and Puppetry* (New York: The Studio Publications, 1958), p. 16.

⁹The languages used in traditional puppetry are discussed in Becker, Brandon, Joan Gross, "Creative Use of Language in a Liège Puppet Theater," *Semiotica*, 47(1/4) (1983), pp. 281-315; Donald Keene, *Major Plays of Chikamatsu* (New York: Columbia University Press, 1961); Michèle Nicolas, "Karagoz: Le Théâtre d'ombres Turc," in *Les Marionnettes*, ed. by Paul Fournel (Paris: Bordas, 1982), pp. 40-55; and Antonio Pasqualino, "Marionettes and Glove Puppets: Two Theatrical Systems of Southern Italy," *Semiotica*, 47(1/4) (1983), pp. 219-280.

¹⁰Recorded in June, 1980 in Washington D.C. at the World Puppetry Festival, with support from the National Endowment for the Humanities and permission of the puppeteers.

¹¹In the sense of Erving Goffman, *Frame Analysis* (New York: Harper and Row, 1974).

¹²Becker, p. 240.

¹³Brandon, p. 62.

¹⁴Gross, p. 307.

¹⁵Blackham, p. 62.

¹⁶Recorded in June, 1980 at the World Puppetry Festival, with permission of the puppeteer.

¹⁷See Goffman. The question of how comical and comical for whom is a complex one. See Pasqualino (this volume).

¹⁸The Liège and Sicilian puppets are related to other twentieth century manifestations and remnants of the medieval troubadour tradition, the Italian *contastorie* and *cantastorie*, which lasted into this century, and the Iberian *cordel* literature, which is read, spoken, and chanted to this day in Brazil.

¹⁹See Becker, p. 240.

²⁰Pasqualino (1983) p. 262.

²¹Frank Whiteman Lindsay, *Dramatic Parody by Marionettes in Eighteenth Century Paris* (New York: King's Crown Press, 1946), pp. 111-112.

²²Léopold Delannoy, *Théâtres de Marionnettes du Nord de la France* (Paris: Maisonneuve & Larose, 1983), p. 10.

²³Ibid., p. 100.

²⁴Punch and Judy examples were recorded in June, 1980 at the World Puppetry Festival with permission of the puppeteer.

²⁵See also discussion in Proschan (1981), pp. 550-551.

²⁶Gross, p. 290.

²⁷Pasqualino (1983), pp. 275-276.

²⁸Examples recorded in June, 1980 at the World Puppetry Festival, with permission of the puppeteer.

²⁹From a performance by the Balinese puppeteer, I. Wayan Wija.

³⁰In fact playwrights such as Federico Garcia Lorca, Michel de Ghelderode, and Alfred Jarry, as well as Futurists and Dadaists, were fascinated by puppets and wrote plays for them.

³¹Our understanding of puppetry has benefited greatly from involvement in the World Puppetry Festival in Washington, D.C. in June 1980 and the International Puppetry Conference and Festival in Palermo, Italy in November, 1983. In particular we have learned much from discussions with Fredrik deBoer, Joan Gross, Kristina Melchior, Antonio Pasqualino, and Frank Proschan.

The Clown Figure in the
Puppet Theatre of West Java:
The Ancestor and the Individual

Kathy Foley

"Who is Semar?" asked an article in the early years of *Djawa*, a magazine devoted to the culture of the Southeast Asian island.[1] Indeed, this clown-servant of the *wayang*, the puppet theatre of the area, has prompted a multitude of answers to this question, as scholars have argued over whether he is indigenous, Indian, or Islamic in origin, an ancient fertility figure or the voice of the common man.[2] Even among the varied comic characters that appear in and, often dominate traditional puppet theatres, Semar seems special. Where figures like Punch play havoc with the social order, slaughtering wives, judges, and hangmen both verbally and literally, the Southeast Asian clown tests ideas of social order in more fundamental ways.[3] Though a originally a high god, he willingly serves a mere man—the hero of whichever tale is told on that particular night. Though his utterances can refer to scatology, sex, or political scandal, they are felt by the audience to contain truths that go beyond such subject matter to hint at a comedy divine.

In form, mythos, and performance usage, his character resolves basic contraditions. He is both male and female; his black body and white face show the mixing of day and night; he represents the peasant and yet is addressed respectfully as "older brother" by princes. When he pops from behind the *kayon* (tree of life) puppet for his first appearance midway in the show, the crowd applauds as the musicians bang raucously on their instruments, calling "Welcome, older Brother Semar." Here and throughout the story, he may, in contrast to the noble characters, talk directly to the musicians and refer to current events that have no relation to the tale.

He breaks all the rules, for he is bigger than all rules. The *dalang's* (puppetmaster) mood song is an apt introduction; the lyrics proclaim: "Semar, Semar, the great figure, the great figure, the great puppet of the screen, body and soul, the bump on his crown (is) the axis of the universe."[4] Who is this puzzling creature?

I will not fully answer here who Semar is—capturing him is beyond the compass of mere mortals who like blindmen define an elephant based on the part of the animal they touch. I will discuss a possible prototype, but know the present day character is more complex, encrusted with centuries of re-interpretation built up as Southeast Asia has assimulated new religions and political systems. Rather the questions I hope to answer are: firstly, who was Semar? What mythos made the clown of the Southeast Asian puppet theatre a more substantive character than his prominent counterparts in other puppet dramas? Secondly, how is Semar? For as Indonesia works out the implications of independence and development, the puppet theatre has, of necessity, experienced changes and the clown has proved especially significant in keeping the genre which I will discuss, the Sundanese *wayang golek purwa* (hereafter, *wayang*), popular. Indeed, my research in 1977-78, 1982, and 1986 has convinced me that an understanding of how Semar and his sons are being interpreted today is central to an understanding of this theatre at present.[5]

Sundanese Wayang Golek Purwa

The Sundanese *wayang golek purwa*, a wooden rod puppet theatre using Sundanese language as its medium and telling stories derived from Hindu epics, is popular in the highlands of West Java, Indonesia.[6] Performances take place primarily in celebration of weddings or circumcisions and are presented outside on a raised stage from 9pm-4:30am in front of the house of the family that has commissioned the performance. The *dalang* (puppetmaster) manipulates all the puppets, sings mood songs, and delivers all the dialogue and narration. He is assisted by one or more female singer (*pasinden*), about ten musicians (*nayaga*) playing on a set of instruments (*gamelan*) composed of metallophones, a wood xylophone, drums, and a bowed lute (*rebab*). This theatre is traditionally dominated by strict typology of character, comprised of five main categories. This system makes it possible for the performer to pick up any of the hundred puppets in the average set and immediately give it a voice and movement appropriate to that type.

Typology of Character

The typology of character is a Sundanese version of the categories of refined and strong that prevails in most Southeast Asian theatre. The five major character types in Sundanese *wayang* are refined (*lemes*), semi-refined (*ladak*), strong (*punggawa*), ogre (*buta*), and special (*khusus*).

Although these catagories can be further sub-divided, they create the framework for all characters who appear in the *wayang*.

Refined characters (*lemes*) have small heads and bodies, their faces are white and downcast. They move in refined walk (*keupat*); their language is laden with polite phrases of old Javanese derivation; and their melodious voices are linked to a low note of the *gamelan* orchestra's scale. A prime example of this type is Arjuna, the middle of the heroic Pandawa brothers of the *Mahabharata* stories.

Semi-refined (*ladak*) characters also have small bodies, but their faces are pink; their gaze, more direct; their movements, swifter and more energetic; their voices, higher and nasal in focus. Their greater ornamentation suggests their wordly nature.

Strong (*punggawa*) characters have larger bodies and eyes; their faces may be blue, dark pink, or yellow. They move in a more bouncing stride (*gedut*). Their language is straight-forward, and their voices are deep and gutteral. Ogres (*buta*) have larger bodies and bulging eyes. Their bodies may be red or other dark shades. They move jerkily and speak distortedly.

For the refined, semi-refined, strong, and ogre characters the movements and voices are essentially the same for all characters within that class. The final class, in contrast, are characters that are "special", i.e. not a class at all, for they do not move or speak according to the rules of a type. They must be learned one at a time, since, in the Sundanese conception, they are one of a kind.[7]

The most important of the fifteen or so characters in this grouping are the *pawongan* (from *wong*-"people"), which include Semar and his three sons (Astrajingga, Dawala, Gareng), and Semar's brother, Togog, with his companion Tokun.[8] Of these characters, Semar, Astrajingga and Dawala, are staples of every Sundanese performance, while Gareng, Togog and Tokun more rarely appear.

Semar has a black body and a white face that rises to a tuft of hair on his forehead. This fat, farty, hermaphroditic character moves in a distinctive, limping walk. His high, whining voice is drawn out on certain syllables, and his jokes degenerate into wisdom. His son Astrajingga, red-bodied and pug-nosed, walks in a loping stride and often does the martial arts (*pecak silat*) dance distinctive to Sunda. His deep voice and "macho" manner contrast with the nasal resonance and more erudite diction of his yellow-hued brother Dawala (sometimes called "penis-nose", due to the prominence of his olfactory apparatus). Dawala walks in mincing step, often hiking up his sarong lest it drag in the dirt. Then comes Gareng in a couple of bouncing steps, and speaks in short retorts. His thoughts are minimal and his vocabulary, mono-syllabic. Togog has a distended lip, from having tried to swallow a mountain in a contest of prowess with Semar, and this explains his stuttering speech. Tokun is more laconic than his companion.

What is most notable about the clowns is not that they are farty or uncouth, but that they are distinctive. For the other types, what the performer attempts to present and what the public reads is a icon of that type. The clowns, outside this typology, represent an individualism that is at a premium in this artistic universe and available only to those at the bottom of the *wayang* world.

Function

Likewise the traditional usage of the *pawongan* helps them to contribute from an individual perspective. When Semar appears in the traditional clown scene, he immediately breaks the epic frame.

As the clown scene opens, Semar, customarily, introduces himself, tells what village he is from (always the village where the *dalang* lives) and thanks those to whom he is grateful, the *guru* of the performer and the host of the evening are most often cited. Next Semar may launch into a speech that promotes family planning or critiques current affairs. The following example, drawn from my field notes, cites the condition of school buildings in the Bandung area and questions the success of the government's "development" program.

> Semar: The government makes buildings, but what use are the buildings if they aren't cared for? Walls crack! Rooves leak! The ground is muddy! They let it be. In 1978 development is supposed to be finished.

Throughout the story, the clowns may make reference to the real world, which the audience inhabits. Astrajingga, in one performance, mocked the pompous speech making of government bureaucrats who call puppeteers in for "up-gradings" to convince the performers to promote government projects.

> Astrajingga: I'm going to practice speech making. (Switching from the local language, Sundanese, to the national language, Indonesian, in which all official communications are promulgated, and adopting a formal tone). Ladies and gentlemen! Male students and female students! Animal tenders and animal tenderizers! . . . Ahem! Dalang are not just entertainment. They are a channel of communication, a mass media. It is the duty of each artist to strengthen his spirit. That is to get hold of himself and stop shaking and aim his aim to the aim of participating in the progress of the country and the development that is our dutiful duty. Whoever counterfeits money. . . .

Arjuna, the white faced hero, is accompanied by the chief clown of Sundanese *wayang golek purwa*, the black-bodied Semar.
Photo: K. Foley

Offerings for an exorcistic performance (*ruwatan*) sit in front of the stage for this Sundanese *wayang golek* presentation. Semar, the chief clown, confronts Kala, a demonic son of the high god of the universe who has gained permission to eat men.

Photo: K. Foley

As these examples intimate, the clown can be used as a transparent mask for the opinions of the particular *dalang* on issues of current concern. While the *dalang* may use the plot or persona of the other puppets to refer metaphorically to current affairs, Semar *is* the *dalang's* voice. The concerns presented are those of the puppetmaster, who in identifying with Semar casts his lot with the commoners who live outside of the pale established by type. Herein lies much of their humor and their strength. They do not adhere to the dreamtime of the narrative in the same way as their masters and can put the battles and bravado into a more pragmatic and comic perspective.

The use of a clown to represent the voice of the common people is a frequent feature of theatrical entertainments especially in class-stratified societies. Shakespeare's Falstaff balances the heroic world-view presented in the Henry plays. Punch, Hanswurst, Kasper, Kargoz and all their clowning cousins have kept the voice of the common man strong in the streets of the West. Yet the commentary of these Western clowns ultimately carries less clout. Where the Western scholars often trace the clown characters back to devils that spewed out of hell mouths of the medieval stage, Semar in the indigenous conception came from heaven. Thus rather than being in a sense devaluated—his communications framed by the fact that he is a "clown" and his statements are "jokes", Semar is ultimately exaulted by the mythos that surrounds this theatre. It is this mythos that lifts the individualism and the humor which might otherwise seem petty toward a more cosmic dimension.

Mythic Origin of Clown

Semar's origin, as understood in Sunda, is reported in the plot of *Sanghyang Rancassan* (The God Rancassan), which tells how Sanghyang Tunggal, the ruler of the universe, had four sons: Ismaya (later Semar), Antaga (later Togog), Rancassan, and Batata Guru (the Hindu Shiva). The father names the youngest, Guru, to succeed him and the handsome Ismaya and Antaga try to persuade the unruly Rancassan to accept Guru as his superior. A fight erupts and Ismaya and Antaga, without intending, rip Rancassan in two and the *layung jamus kalimasadah*, the heirloom treasure which brings peace and fertility to the country its owner rules, falls from his head.

For the fratricide they are sent into the world. Ismaya transforms into Semar to carry the heirloom to the earth where he will lend it to the righteous rulers he serves. Togog descends to serve the ogre kings who will challenge Semar's masters. Semar, reluctant to travel alone, looks at his shadow which becomes Astrajingga. Togog conceives Tokun as his side-kick. As Semar descends to earth he strikes the wind with the *layung jamus kalimasadah*, begetting Dawala and Gareng.

As a god who is *sakti mandraguna* (magically potent), Semar can incarnate as a male or a female, transform himself or others into divine form, or see through any ruse others try. And yet rather than exert his power to seize power, in traditional stories he and his sons usually appear only in conjunction with the hero—most often, the refined knight Arjuna. After the midnight clown scene in which Semar and his sons depart freely from the plot for up to an hour, traditional stories return to the exploits of this hero in his never-ending struggle with ogres.[9]

The clowns act here much as fools in Elizabethan comedy or side-kicks in TV or the movies. They offer support, advice, and infuse humor into the plot that centers on the noble character. As their master fights ogre kings, fending them off with deft flips of the wrist and kicks, the clowns fell the low class ogres by farting in their faces or bashing their stomach with boxing gloves, until the ogres vomit forth streams of spagetti on their heads.

Though techniques of evoking laughter remain the same, modern stories which have become a major part of the repertory since 1945 are allowed much freer use of these devices because the clowns have more plot focus and, hence, playing time. In 22 of 51 stories that I studied by attending performances and listening to commercially available cassettes of popular *dalang* in 1978, the clowns were the central figures presented and floated freely through the plot from evening till morning. In *The Knight Sukmasajati*, for instance, instead of seeking to kill Arjuna, the ogres resolve to kill one of the clowns. In *The Knight Suryaningrat* instead of a princess falling in love with a hero, she longs to wed one of Semar's sons. Only at the conclusion of the tale will the clown be reunited with Arjuna, who in traditional stories would dominate the plot. During my initial study of this theatre in 1977-78, I attributed this usurpation of plot by the clown to the expectations that democracy established in the mind of the common man and the growing individualism that was being cultivated in post-World War II Indonesian society. Mythic mediators like Arjuna, I felt, were being replaced by the clowns who were representative of ordinary citizens. Only after almost ten years of playing traditional stories as a puppeteer myself have I come to sense the deep irony of this independent clown.

Though I have emphasized the voice of the clown as "individual" and introduced him as a special case, I believe that this individualism is itself a mask of a much older and more penetrating conception of the human psyche and social relations. This understanding probably comes from an archaic layer of Malay culture and helps explain the veneration of the clowns as of godly origin. The joke is that the hero and his clowns are inseperable in traditional stories because, in reality, they are the component parts of one person: the complete self in indigenous thought. This self is a five-fold being—a person and his spirit siblings, the "four brothers/sisters."[10] Though my evidence is fragmentary, I believe even a preliminary presentation can be useful in showing this possible origin of Semar and explaining why other god-clowns of other puppet theatres remain dwarfed by him.

The "four siblings" (dulur opat)

In Sundanese, as in Javanese and Balinese thought, we do not come alone into the world. Rather we are accompanied by important companions—the blood that is the first sign of labor, the water that spills as our birthsack breaks, the placenta that is born with us, and the umbilical cord are our brothers/sisters, and they continue, as our spirit guardians, to have impact on our life.[11] The blood and water, because they disappear, receive less attention than the most powerful sibling, the afterbirth, and the secondarily important umbilical cord.

The afterbirth with due funeral rites is normally buried in a coconut shell near the house shortly after birth. People say if something untoward happened to the afterbirth, so it will happen to the child. Sickness and unhappiness occur when a person somehow neglects his spirit brothers, the afterbirth in particular. A long and happy life results from proper relations with them.

Nor is this afterbirth a static entity, for some say that each pregnancy of a woman is the return of the spirit of that same afterbirth to her womb. Thus the individual and his real siblings are, conceptually, all united in that they are materializations of the powerful afterbirth.

In a larger dimension, this afterbirth figure that dies to give us life is somehow associated with the idea of "ancestor." As the afterbirth is buried with honors, and remains the source of luck and life for the individual, so to the grave of a noted progenitor of the village is the symbolic power center for the villages in West Java that follow old tradition. The fate of the current generation is felt to be tied to the former generations, and, if the spirit of the ancestor is neglected, the living will suffer too. Harvest offerings are brought to such grave sites to gain good luck and fertility,[12] Thus in the great round of things, the afterbirth and the ancestor symbolically reminds the individual that all living in one place are united by their common origin, and the individual's power stems from this chthonic other more powerful and permanent than himself.

The umbilicus is second in importance and is preserved in a small sack along with medicinal herbs. (When possible, ground which absorbed the water and blood spilt at the baby's birth are put in the sack too.) In the house where I lived in 1977-78, this sack was often waved over the baby to prevent disease—an action which I often found repeated in *wayang* stories like *Brajamusti* where queen Arimbi revives her dead child by moving the sack over his body. In Stories like *Rengganis*, from the Amir Hamzah repertory, a king will lie sick as his country is beseiged, until someone strikes his attackers with an arrow making them reveal their real identity—the king's afterbirth, umbilicus, water and blood. He was at odds with his four siblings! The umbilicus, I believe, is an outward sign of this continuing connection with the afterbirth/ancestor. When disease or distress strike, people pull out the umbilical cord to remind themselves and the powerful afterbirth/ancestor of the covenent between them.

In a larger dimension, the idea of the umbilical cord is significant as well. Capitals are often felt to be navels of the earth, places where the actions of the most powerful ancestors can still feed power to those living now. In a lesser dimension, each village is a center tapping into the power of the local hero-ancestor. The villages that practice old Sundanese traditions for welcoming the new year have a ceremony in which the head of the village customarily begins a walk from the center of the village to the perimeter of the village in the four directions. This journey inscribes the area in which the ancestor feeds power to the living— the distance the umbilicus of that particular ancestor "stretches."

Traditional practices concerning the four siblings and ceremonies for the ancestors are carried out today without any firm understanding of meaning by participants, but the idea of the four siblings is still embedded in the culture. And the special treatment accorded the afterbirth is common in Malay societies from Malaysia to the Philippines.

Proverbs like "the four brothers and the fifth as center" (*dulur opat kalima pancer*) are commonly heard, if dimly understood. In this proverb, the brothers are thought of as the four points of the compass, with the *pancer* (the fifth—the child) as center. Although in daily life the individual is the only perceived member of the group, this invisible support system keeps each person in balance.[13]

I believe that the clowns in Sunda are these same spirit brothers. Semar is the afterbirth—and hence the crucial sibling who must accompany the child, the hero of the story. This clarifies the distorted shape, the god-like powers of Semar, and his persistence in every lakon. Astrajingga, the oldest son and the most important clown after his father, is the umbilical cord. Dawala and Gareng represent the water and the blood. Hence in the stories the clowns are the constants—the brothers representing the ancestor while the hero—the child—is always changing.

Although it may seem strange that what appears in a puppet play to be a hero (Arjuna) accompanied by comic sidekicks (Semar and sons) is in actuality a representation of the individual (baby) and the chthonic powers that create him and protect him through life (afterbirth, water, blood, unbilicus), I would argue that this is the mythos behind. This corresponds with the interpretations which *dalang* place on the opening scene as birth of the child, the first battle of the night as adolescent testing, and the final battle as the confrontation with death. The reason that four clowns is the favored number in Java is that they represent the four brothers, who follow each in life and who physicalize the periphery to create the child as center. The mystical implications of this system of centering are complex, for the brothers are the four directions, the elements, the humors, the days of the Javanese week, and much more. But the core is the mystery of the self: the one in five that is a combination of the oldest, the most powerful, the uglist being, the afterbirth/ancestor (Semar); and the youngest, the most fragile, the most beautiful being, the baby/hero (Arjuna).

This integral connection of the clown and the hero, in Southeast Asian thought has been expanded from the microcosm of the individual into the macrocosmic dimension. Hence, Semar and his sons are considered the commoners and moving in conjuction with the rightful king. Although the hero seems autonomous, the traditional stories constantly remind us that he is ultimately puny compared to his servants who save him with advice and action when great danger rises, and even the right to rule derives from the heirloom Semar and his sons bestow. The idea that common people create the center of power—the ruler— is apparent. As the mythos of the four brothers and the mystic interpretations of their part in the life of the individual (as represented by the hero) have faded from the collective consciousness, it is this more rational, class interpretation of the clown that has come to predominate. As a representative of the peasantry, he puts the heroics into the little guy's perspective. The result is paradoxical—the clown is at once an archaic figure, the eternally present ancestor, and the most modern and flexible element of the show, the individualistic spokesperson for today's villager.

How is Semar?

How then are we to interpret modern plots in which the clowns do not appear in conjunction with the aristocratic hero and have themselves usurped the plot? A representative story is *Suryaningrat* in which a beautiful princess begs her father to bring her the beloved she has seen in a dream, the clown Dawala.

The Kurawa, the traditional opponents of the Pandawa heroes in *The Mahabharata* seek to prevent the marriage. The normally heroic Arjuna, acting under the influence of the jealous Kurawa, kills Dawala for allegedly stealing his heirloom treasure. Dawala with the aid of his godly ancestors becomes the handsome knight Suryaningrat and avenges himself on the Kurawa and Arjuna. Finally, Dawala returns to his original shape and finds the princess is, in actuality, the missing heirloom.

In traditional stories, Arjuna would be winning the battles and marrying the princesses and the major battles might be between Arjuna and ogres from an overseas kingdom. In the story above, the clown fights the Kurawa and his own master, Arjuna. Though the traditional relationship of clown and hero is restored at the end of the play, the balance is tenuous. The myth of interdependence of commoner and ruler has eroded. The rulers are, in *Suryaningrat*, portrayed as persecuting the clowns, forgetting that the clowns are a part of them, forgetting that without the strength of the periphery, the commoners, they are not a center. I have argued elsewhere that the ascendency of the clowns represents the rise of the new democratic order and the implied critique of the ruler in stories like that above may result from the devaluation of the traditional aristocracy that was begun by the declaration of a republican form of government,[14] The myth of the benevolent ruler has been further tested by the Indonesian government's inability to meet the villagers' expectations. Although it is clear that the change in sociopolitical circumstances has led to a decline in the mythos of kings and servants, a kind of irony remains. The mythos of a mystically interwoven universe of siblings is crumbling. This idea allowed an individual to approach positively parts of his psyche which were elemental—the farts, sex, the foolishness of life. It allowed people to see the village ways as the source of life and appreciate the fact that these ways are older and more powerful and a prerequiste for the refined figures and kingly governments we present to the world. Changing ideas of the self and the social order are being ushered in by education. Belief in a spirit world is fading, at the same time that migration to the city is snapping the conceptual cords that bind one villager to another. Wage labor is supplanting a concept of mutual help among villagers—in the modern world it is every clown for himself.

Notes

[1]J. Kats, *Djawa* 3 (1923), p. 55.

[2]L. Serrurier in *De Wajang Poerwa: Eene Ethnologische Studie* (Leiden: E.J. Brill, 1896), argued he was an Indonesian version of the *vidusaka*, the clown of Sankrit drama (p. 93). G.A.J. Hazeu in *Bijdrage tot de Kennis van het Javaansche Toneel* (Leiden: E.J. Brill, 1897) saw the clown as a representative of the original Javanese ancestors (p. 112). A traditional Javanese deity said Boediarja in *Djawa* 2, 1, p.xx; a representation of Islamic ideas (Moesa, "Grepen uit de Wajang, in Verband met den Islam" *Djawa* 3 [1923], pp. 56-62); an ancient fertility god of indigenous (E.W.

Maurenbrecher, "De Panakawan-figuren in de Cheribonsche Wajang" *Djawa* 19 [1939], pp. 187-196) or Indian puppet theatre origin (J.J. Ras, "De Clownfiguren in de Wajang" *Bijdragen tot de Taal-, Land-, en Volkenkunde* 134 [1978], pp. 451-465); a representation of the Javanese people in contrast to their rulers (H.O., "Petruk als Vorst" *Djawa* 2 [1922], pp. 170); a trickster figure said C.P. Eskamp *Semar as Trickster: Wayang as a Multi-classificatory Representation of Javanese Society* (Leiden: Instituut voor Anthropologie en Sociologie der Neit Westerse Volken, Rijksuniversiteit Leiden, 1976). In conversations I have heard people claim he is a shaman or a representative of the negritos that inhabited Java prior to the arrival of Malayo-Polynesian peoples, and in practice I have been given love charms that evoke him, since he is also linked to the god of love. After sorting through a wide variety of opinions by Indonesian and Dutch scholars, Sri Mulyono gave his judgement—Semar is a spiritual guide to point people to the correct path (Sri Mulyono Joyosupadmo, *Wayang: Asal-usul, Filsafat dan Masa Depannya* [Jakarta: B.P. Alda, 1975]).

[3]Semar is the clearest and perhaps the oldest articulation of the god-clown puppet figure of Southeast Asia. His cousins, who have comparable features, include The Balinese clown Tawlen, Pak Dogel of the Malay Wayang Kulit Siam, Ayang in the Cambodian theatre of the same name.

[4]"*Semar 2 ya gegelar wayang agung kelir nagraga sukma, Semar kuncung pakuing alam.*" *Padalangan di Pasundan* (Bandung: Yayasan Pusat Olah Seni Pawayangan, 1977), p. 9, my translation based on interview with my teacher Gunawan Djayakusumah. Exact translation of mood songs is difficult because they are derived from middle Javanese and have been passed for a number of generations through an oral tradition by Sundanese speakers who have altered parts and only dimly understand the meanings.

[5]See my "Clown in the Sundanese Wayang Golek: Democratization of a Feudal Ethos," *Scenarium* 9, 1985: pp. 88-99 for a fuller discussion of changes in treatment of the clowns.

[6]The form as practiced today was created about 150 years ago by puppeters from the northern coast of Java who migrated into the area and began to tell Hindu-based stories with wooden figures that they earlier told with shadow puppets. Features which distinguish current Sundanese *wayang golek purwa* from the better known central Javanese *wayang kulit purwa* are the use of a single tuning system for instruments, the five tone *salendo* scale; the prominence accorded the female singers; the free interjection of comments by the musicians during a performance; a looser performance structure; different interpretations of the classical stories of a roughly comparable repertory; and a generally livelier performance style. Javanese form can be considered more refined, court-oriented, subtle and subdued, while Sundanese is more lively, village-oriented, straightforward and brash.

[7]In studying this puppet genre, I found this contention not completely true. A number of the characters in this class do use similar movement patterns though energy usage and mannerisms personalize the movement and each voice is distinct. Also, although Sundanese class all ogres together, individual *dalang* are currently inventing new ogres of lower class (*buta biasa* ("ordinary ogre")) which they endow with distinctive vocal and movement mannerisms. Structurally speaking, these ogres are in this "special" class. Such new ogres show this individualized category is an area of growth in current *wayang*.

[8]These characters are sometimes called *punakawan* as in central Java. Semar and Togog are equivalent to the Javanese characters of the same names. Dawala is Petruk, the second son of Semar in Javanese *wayang*. Gareng is comparable to the oldest son of Semar in the Javanese wayang, but in Sunda he is the youngest son. Astrajingga or Cepot is considered Semar's eldest child in Sunda, and may be related to the Javanese Bagong, Semar's youngest son. Tokun is equivalent to Sarahita in Java.

[9]This pattern of clowns emerging around midnight for the clown scene then following along with the hero for the remainder of the night is standard in Javanese theatre as well. In Balinese shadow theatre, where the clowns are needed throughout the story to translate the archaic language of their master into the vernacular, they appear from the outset of the story, but still in conjunction with the more noble characters.

[10]For the most complete discussion of the four siblings in English see C. Hooykaas, *Cosmogony and Creation in Balinese Tradition* (the Hague, Martinus Nijhoff, 1974). He relates the symbology to Buddhism, and there is no doubt that Buddhism has played a part in the conceptualization of the siblings as the gods of the four directions in relation to the central creator. I would argue, however, that an older idea of spirit brothers was consolidated with the Buddhist mythos. I base this opinion on the fact that the childbirth, ancestor veneration ideas I discuss in this essay seem not to be practiced in India, but are a feature of many Malay groups.

[11]See *Upacara Tradisional Daerah Jawa Barat* (Jakarta: Departement Pendidikan dan Kebudayaan, 1981/2), p. 52-58 for a concise explication of these childbirth customs as practiced among the Sundanese.

[12]Ronny Usman in "Mapag Sri," *Kawit* 12 (2-3), p. 13-15 reports on such ceremonies in Slangit near Cirebon. There *wayang kulit purwa* performances are a vital part of ceremonies for celebrating the rice harvest. In the midst of a puppet play held annually at the graves of the ancestors, the performance is halted to formally give offerings to the village ancestors, the holy water made during this ceremony is then given to audience members especially the young men and women from in front of the grave. The connection of wayang, the ancestor figure, and fertility seems clear.

[13]If Hookyaas is right in *Cosmogony and Creation*, much of this directional imagery is imported from India. If this is the case, it may be an explanation why Semar, as ancestor/afterbirth, is so much more important than the other clowns. It is possible that the idea of an ancestor whose energy was made available to men in a vertical dimension (from below, through fertility in the earth where burial took place, and from above where the spirit of the ancestor might float until it returned to earth) was spread out to the four directions. This might also explain why the afterbirth is always important in Malay cultures, but the idea of four rather than one, or two, or three siblings is strong only where Hindu culture has been strong— Java, Bali, and Sunda.

This fivefold idea become pervasive in *Sanghyang Rancassan* with its four figures grouped around a focal character. A single, central god (Tunggal) yields four sons. Then Semar and Togog leave heaven to the new central figure, the new high god (Guru), and thereupon they each get a companion to bring the number up to the required four. Later, when Semar and Astrajingga split off from Togog and Sarita, Semar creates two new sons so that the new foursome can surround the new center, the hero.

[14]See note 5.

Functions of the Comic Attendants (*Panasar*) in a Balinese Shadowplay

Fredrik E. deBoer

In the last few years, a body of research has begun to accumulate that allows us to understand the fascinating theater of Bali, and especially the *wayang kulit*, or shadow puppet play, in much greater detail than was formerly possible. Scripts of *wayang* plays in translation and full performance transcriptions are becoming available, and thorough descriptions and detailed analyses of the form have been published. Consideration of the medium may now proceed with reference to specific examples.[1] In the present paper I shall discuss the functional tasks of an important group of stock characters in Balinese *wayang kulit*, with reference to a single, exemplary, performance: "The Death of Kumbakarna", as performed by the late *dalang* (master puppeteer) I Ketut Madra of Sukawati village on August 10, 1977.[2]

Even the earliest writers on Bali's shadow theater emphasized the importance of four comic attendant characters, the *panasar* (literally "basic characters") who play very prominent roles in every South Balinese *wayang parwa* (devoted to the Mahabharata-based repertoire) or *wayang ramayana* (devoted to the Ramayana) performance. These sometimes wise buffoons, cousins to the sacred clowns found in the puppet theaters of neighboring Java and mainland South East Asia, are low-caste commoners in appearance and behavior, although they are credited by legend with divine origin.[3]

Two of them, fat old Tualen and his quick-witted son Mredah, always serve the virtuous party in the *wayang* story, while pompous, conceited Delem and his sly, ironical brother Sangut are invariably present on the side of the villains or antagonists. Rather than taking the stage for particular sections of the *wayang* play as their Javanese counterparts do, the Balinese *panasar* are in nearly constant attendance on their masters throughout the evening and occupy the screen for more than half the total running time. Humor and comedy in Balinese *wayang* are left almost entirely to them.[4]

The characterizations of these beloved favorites are quite firmly set by tradition and are not subject to experimentation or redefinition by the *dalang*; like many well-established film stars in pre-War Hollywood, the *panasar* do not alter from play to play or from one director (*dalang*) to another. Tualen is always slow, deep-voiced, staunch, Mredah quick and high-pitched, Delem hotheaded, Sangut sly. Any Balinese villager knows them all by appearance and voice. However, the specific gags, jokes, similes, witty observations, pranks and so on which make up the "material" with which the *panasar* work, are very much the individual creation of the particular *dalang*, and the quality of this material is an important measure of the puppeteer's ability to entertain.

In the paragraphs that follow a series of specific examples illustrating the work of the *panasar* shall be given, including every bit of comedy that provoked audible laughter from the audience at the performance under consideration, in the order in which they occurred. Taken together, the examples give a fairly complete picture of the work of the *panasar* in Balinese *wayang* more generally.

1

DELEM: (*Enters from the right, bowing and scraping, as the music continues. Audience laughter.*)

The audience laughs when Delem appears for the first time. He bustles hastily into the audience chamber, exhibiting a demeanor that is in complete contrast to the stately, dance-like locomotion of the principal characters who have come in before him. His appearance is grotesque—he has a large goitre—and he moves in a jerky, darting manner, his head shaking. The laughter that greets him represents more an expression of recognition and a delighted anticipation of good fun than a response to anything specifically funny about his behavior at this time. This moment of entrance also provides a opportunity for the audience to contemplate his look and personal style.

It is a small comic passage focussed entirely on who the clown is, rather than on what he does, a momentary interposition into a surrounding scene which is quite serious and elevated in tone. Sangut's entrance a few lines later receives a similar reaction, and passes by equally quickly.

2

DELEM: (*Laughing nervously as he comes forward to interpret. When he speaks, his mouth moves and his eyes flash.*) Ha, ha,ha! Yessir, my Lord, yessir Your Highness! Please excuse me now, for I will

interpret Your Highness' words to him, Your Highness' younger
brother, who has just approached you, isn't that true?
Please witness that I am paying my respects, that I be not to be
struck by your curse as I interpret Your Highness' thoughts.
(*He bows and turns to address* KUMBAKARNA.)
Ah, yessir, My Lord, attend to the words of your elder brother who is
"Umbrella of the Country" [that is to say, the protector of the people]
here in Alengka...."

The high-status "Hindu" characters in a Balinese shadow play,
whether heroes, villains, ogres or monkeys, speak the ancient Kawi
language, a form of Old Javanese which is not understood by many
of those in the typical audience. To help the spectators understand, the
panasar interpret (*ngojah* "imitate, echo") the words of their masters
into colloquial Balinese on a running basis as the action proceeds. Hence
they are always near at hand when their masters might wish or need
to talk.

Before one of the *panasar* is free to interpret on behalf of his master,
he requests permission to do so, as part of the essential series of formalities
included at the beginning of every Balinese *wayang* play. Thereafter
he is at liberty to provide a running translation and to comment without
fear of censure. He is thus granted explicit permission to break and
otherwise play with prevailing social codes, and an important part of
the humor generated during the performance will arise from his officially
sanctioned transgressive behavior. Paradoxically however, the *panasar*
also serve to preserve and maintain the traditional court etiquette within
the contemporary Balinese image stream. It has, after all, been many
years since a traditional feudal court of the kind that is modelled in
Rawana's Alengka has been operational on Bali, and most spectators
are familiar with that milieu only through the theater.

This following example of the *panasar* in his function as interpreter
is one of many which might be drawn from the first Audience Scene
(known as the *pagunem* or *patangkilan*), a part of the *wayang* play
in which discussion is the predominant element.
[In the examples that follow, speeches in the Kawi language are rendered
in boldface type; singing is indicated by use of *italics*. All levels of the
Balinese language and the occasional Indonesian words and short phrases
are printed in ordinary type.]

KUMBAKARNA: (*in Kawi, to* RAWANA) You order Kumbakarna to
depart for battle. Useless! Will you be pleased if my corpse is
presented to Rama as an offering on the battlefield?

SANGUT: (*in Balinese*) Just now you tell me to prepare to face the enemy there on the battlefield. Not me! I won't go with you. I won't fight against Lord Rama! In fact now there's no way I'll stay in one piece. If you order me to go, I can do it, but I'll lose. Really. Don't expect me to be able to defeat Lord Rama.

Following every successful "transmission" the high character confirms the accuracy of the translation:

KUMBAKARNA: Indeed!
SANGUT: Right!

The atomic unit or basic building block of a scene involving dialogue is made from four component parts: speech by "high" character in Kawi, translation/elaboration of the speech in Balinese, confirmation, reconfirmation. The first part is rarely more than a few phrases long, while the second is flexible in length, depending on the degree of elaboration; the final pair is always the same four syllables: "Yogya! Patut!"

But the attendants do not often serve merely to provide a kind of auditory subtitle by exactly restating what has been uttered in the old sacral language; as the example given above already suggests, the *panasar* often develop and elaborate on their master's expression as they "follow Your Lordship's thought" (*ngiring pakayunan palungguh cokoridewa*). Sangut elaborates, exemplifies, contextualizes, and refines his superior's words and thoughts. He lends majesty and dignity to his utterance by singing appropriate quotations (and sometimes pseudo-quotations!) from the ancient literature. His speech is different from that of his master, not only in vocabulary and syntax, but in the abundance presence of paralinguistic modifiers: expletives, vocalized pauses, grunts, gestures, mannerisms, pacing about, looking forward and backward. The Kawi speaker tends to be both direct and general, while his attendant is at once circuitous and particular.

3

[DELEM'S *principal*, RAWANA, *grows angry with* KUMBAKARNA, *who is attended by* SANGUT. DELEM *echoes* RAWANA's *rage.*]
DELEM: Aiiitt!!! It gives me a pain in the chest! (*He spits on* KUMBAKARNA.) Ptuii!!!
SANGUT: Good lord! A wad of spit as big as an egg! Right here in front of the king! (*Audience laughter.*)

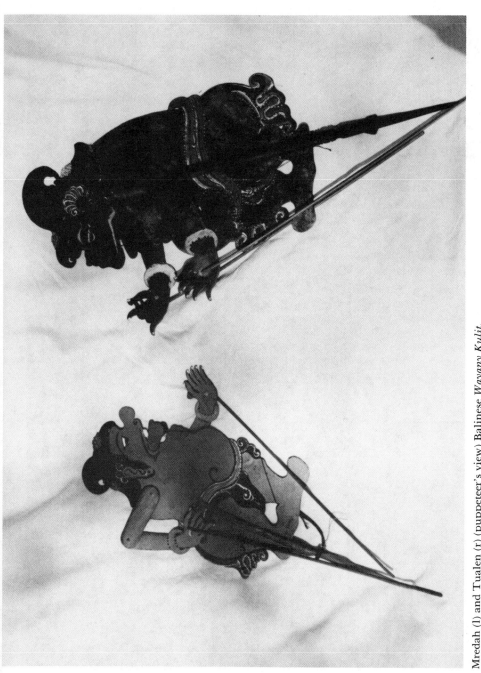

Mredah (l) and Tualen (r) (puppeteer's view) Balinese *Wayang Kulit*.
Photo: F. deBoer

Sangut and Delem (rt). Balinese Wayang Kulit

Balinese Wayang Kulit. From left, Sangut, Delem, Tualen, Mredah.
Photo: F. deBoer

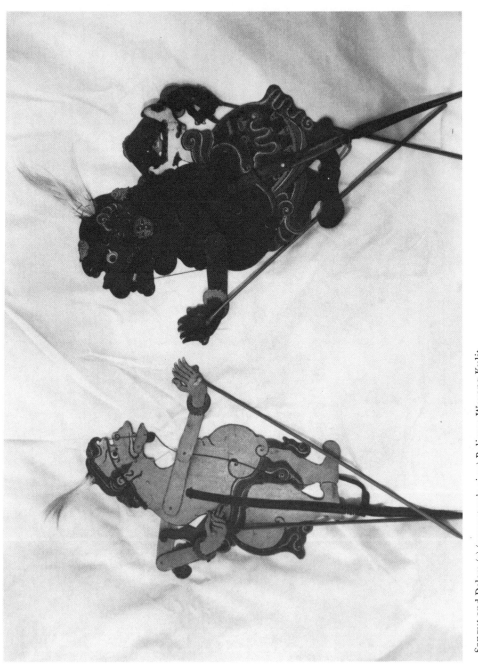

Sangut and Delem (r) (puppeteer's view) Balinese Wayang Kulit.
Photo: F. deBoer

Mredah (l.) and Tualen (rt.) Balinese Wayang Kulit.

Photo: F. deBoer

Although he is an ogre RAWANA is too stately and dignified to do so crass a thing as spit at his brother. DELEM delights the audience by knowing no such restraint and at the same time offers a delightful glimpse of a situation in which the commoner is allowed to insult royalty. Nevertheless, the license granted to Delem is strictly a delegated one, and the *panasar* is never insolent to his own master. Even skeptical Sangut, who may venture a comic aside that is cynical about the chances of the party he serves, is not openly disrespectful to his own boss.

4

DELEM: [About your mighty powers]...Don't keep them hidden away like gold and jewels in a box—later on you might not find the key.

Delem embellishes Rawana's expression of demands with a well-known figure of speech. The Balinese language tradition is extremely rich in sayings, maxims, proverbs, riddles, and word play, as Swellengrebel (1950-52) documented. These pre-existing formulations provide a kind of humorous delight even when they are not explicitly funny.

5

In the next example, Sangut draws a wry and witty twist from the convention of etiquette by which the King is often traditionally referred to as the "Umbrella of the Country (*tedung jagat*), likening him as umbrella to a burnt and limbless tree. Kumbakarna works with his deputy in extending the trope:

SANGUT: The reason a king is called the "Umbrella of his Country" is that all the people in the country need him, need his shelter when it gets hot for them. That's the responsibility of a king.
KUMBAKARNA: They are like deer who take shelter beneath a burnt tree. Where shall they find great comfort?
SANGUT: That's how it is when one puts trust in selfish greed, as you do. But you still want to rule the country, to be in charge of the world. What will happen to the people of the country then? When the world and the people need shelter, will they try to find shade under a tree that is broken and burnt? That's what your way is like!
KUMBAKARNA: As with the desire of a deer to take shade beneath a burnt tree, it is impossible to get comfort there.

SANGUT: It's no different from a deer who has the idea to shade himself beneath a burnt and broken tree. Where does it say that he will get comfort? He will only meet with misfortune and suffering without end.

This example also demonstrates the contribution of the *panasar*'s repetition to the theatrical impact of the scene. As he speaks in alternation with his master, Sangut seconds and prompts him, giving increased urgency to Kumbakarna's point and a sense of "build" to the scene's development. And, apart from giving the teller an opportunity to gather his resources for the next bit of forward narrative motion, the repeating serves to ensure that all of the audience members, who sit in a noisy environment, are given a good opportunity to comprehend what is said.

6

DELEM: (*to* KUMBAKARNA) You're so clever at flapping your jaw, why your tongue doesn't have a bone in it.

Sarcasm, as much as other forms of impudence, is normally quite out of bounds for the Balinese commoner speaking to those of high status. Once again, Delem delights his (predominantly commoner) audience by transgressing established codes. Here he employs a favorite simile, frequently used to describe an excessively smooth talker, one whose tongue is too supple. Something similar might be conveyed by the English "Why butter wouldn't melt in your mouth!"

***

Another example:

DELEM: You're an enemy. Don't you pinch me and squeeze me when I'm not looking. You love like a body louse [sucking blood with a smile].

These similes draw not laughter but grunts of recognition from the audience. They amuse but are not set up as jokes. In the second case, the final part of the expression is so well-known to his audience that Sangut does not even need to complete the phrase.

7

During a break in the Audience Scene action, Sangut, alone, has been talking about the Law of Divine Retribution (*karmapala*):

SANGUT: If you plant a yam, you'll pick a yam; he who enjoys the planting will harvest the fruit (*He laughs*).

The proverb, saying, or adage is another type of traditional verbal formulation found in the play. This proverbial expression, equivalent in meaning to "You will reap just what you sow" is offered as a wise maxim, and lends the stature of traditional authority to Sangut's point of view. A superb rhetorician, he persuades by precept and example.

8

The audience scene concludes with Kumbakarna's agreeing to go to the battlefield, and the principals leave the screen. The *panasar* then recapitulate what has happened, and complete the exposition of necessary information. At this point also, released from any behavioral constraints imposed by proper decorum in the presence of royalty, they are free to give vent to their own thoughts and emotions without restraint. The results are broadly exaggerated expressions of feeling that are the more comic for their quick alteration.

DELEM: Think of the members of the family. How many of them were killed by the monkeys? Oh, Sangut, oh, oh, oh.
(DELEM *weeps bitterly for a moment at the thought. Then he grows angry.*)
   Too insolent! They don't know that they're just monkeys! It's gone to the point where they've killed off the king's generals!
   Keep in mind, I'm sorry about Lord Prahasta, Sangut. He was killed by a little monkey, the son of Sugriwa. Sugriwa has a son, what do you call him? Lord Nila. Every time I think about it, I want to destroy them, destroy them!
(DELEM *gesticulates wildly to show what he might do to the monkeys. In his excitement he hits* SANGUT *in the neck. Audience laughter*).
SANGUT; Ouch! Hey, that hurt my neck! (*Audience laughter.*)

This exchange, being a proper comic sequence, is carefully structured and timed. The first laugh is set off by Delem's being carried away into throwing a whirlwind of blows, and the louder laugh that ends the little routine is inspired by Sangut's perfectly timed "take", pause, and response to Delem's blow. A miniature comic "bit" like this one may be thought of as belonging to the puppeteer rather than to the larger tradition of Balinese shadow puppetry. Every puppeteer has many little sequences of this kind in his repertoire, and although he may borrow from the work of his predecessors and contemporaries, the originality of his jokes and gags is an important consideration in public opinion of his talent.

DELEM: What can [mere] monkeys do? Bah! Grr! We'll peel off Sugriwa's pelt, Sangut!

SANGUT: (Speaking about DELEM) Wow! What's he saying? This's what they call a blockhead. This fellow makes me itch.

Very often Delem and Sangut work together as a comic team, alternatively serving in the roles of comedian and straightman. The essential contrast between their personalities serves to motivate extended byplay. Even when the forward motion of the plot slows to allow for exposition, bickering between two *panasar* keeps the scene lively. Delem always tends to be hotheaded and enthusiastic in support of his wicked master, while Sangut tries to introduce a more sensible perspective.

In the following section, Sangut addresses the audience directly by means of an aside. Delem has been bragging about what he will do to the monkeys.

SANGUT: Bah! Right away he's jumping up and down. First he builds up his energy and then he can't act normal. Truly a guy with very ordinary knowledge, that's Delem. As soon as he gets two bits in his pocket he thinks he's rich and changes his hair style. Three days later he can't buy coffee, and there's nothing left in his mustache but dirt. Wow, what a guy!

Sangut's characterization of Delem is fixed firmly in the everyday life of village Bali and indexes a more contemporary set of spatial and temporal references than those locating the action of the protagonists in the play. Boundaries between the disparate realms of high/ancient and low/modern are by no means distinct, however, for they interpenetrate and blend together to create a multidimensional reality.

10

An important function of the *panasar* is to convey the intellectual content and didactic messages of the play. Again the paradigms are typically drawn from village living and find expression in traditional similes and images. Parables and fables are the favored means of expression, as in this example, in which Sangut praises humility and knowing one's place:

SANGUT: Delem, cut down your big ideas! It's easy for you to have big ideas. Let me tell you, I think we should be like the little paddy bird. Yep! His feathers are dirty, he doesn't like to fly at all, and he never flies higher than his friends. He's content to fly very low.

If he wants food, he only eats grass, even the fallen leaves. Do you think he's picky? Why is he that way? Because he thinks about what's what, Mr. Paddy Bird does.

So why do you act so carelessly? You know the value of life. We don't just live in order to eat; food is only something to keep us alive. We need to have high knowledge, for how can we have a life that is high if our knowledge is low?

DELEM: Who are you talking about?

SANGUT: Mr. Paddy Bird, he has ideas like that.

DELEM: Does Mr. Paddy Bird want to have his face flattened, like yours?

(DELEM *raps on* SANGUT's *flat nose for emphasis. Audience laughter.*)

As Delem pokes his brother on the nose, the *dalang* raps sharply with a gavel he holds between the toes of his right foot against the hard wooden side of his puppet chest, to punctuate, give emphasis, and trigger the laughter. The practice is very reminiscent of the "rimshots" on the snare drum which formerly served a similar purpose in American burlesque theater.

***

In another instance of a didactic lesson drawn from homely examples in village life, Sangut presses Delem to better weigh his words:

SANGUT: Delem, when you speak you should say something worthwhile. Don't be like the *"kukul kubu"* [the little clapper in a shack in the rice field that scares away birds]. You know, "tung, tung, tung", it gets struck a thousand times daily, how many people pass by? Nobody pays any attention to it. That's called a voice without value, those are many sounds without value.

If you're looking for a voice *with* value, the one who seldom speaks, that's the one. Like the *"kukul banjar"* [the big slit drum in the neighborhood that sounds the alarm when there are thieves or a fire breaks out.] One "TUNG," like that! No matter how busy they are, people stop working, "What's going on in the neighborhood?

11

After the recapitulation and discussion which follows the Audience Scene, Kumbakarna and his army of ogres make ready to depart. Sangut is left alone for a time, and he speaks even more honestly.

SANGUT: (*Alone*) If I think about it to myself, even though he's going to battle, we're not going to win. (*He laughs sadly*) Oh dear! That's how strong the monkeys are. Why, there were a thousand monkeys, and a thousand are still left. There were a million ogres and its like a million are already dead. Finished, that's how it feels.

It would be better if we found a lot more troops. Although Rama has only a few monkeys there, they are the best of the best, knights among knights, brave as can be, tremendously strong. Here we've got a lot of terrifying generals, but they only *look* fierce, with their long fangs—they're all second-hand. (*Audience laughter.*)

Sangut gets a modest chuckle from the audience in response to an incongruity between the thought of mythic Old Javanese—speaking ogres with long, sharp fangs and the modern (in Bali) notion of selling at second hand.

More importantly, he takes on something like the task of the chorus in the ancient Greek tragedy: he represents the common sense point of view of the low-caste villagers, who leave deeds of noble valor to their superiors. Sangut's doubts are generic, inevitable, inherent in his character and his dramatic function.

12

Before the ogre horde can actually depart for the front, Kumbakarna must be installed as battle commander. Sangut calls upon the women of the court to bring offerings for the ceremony and then to dance in honor of the occasion.

SANGUT (*Hesitates for a moment, then calls off screen to the women servants.*) Hey, all you women, get going! Spread out the offerings. What's happening? Where are the offerings for the installation of the Commander in Chief? He's going off to war! It won't do to be careless, remember the offerings to present in the temple.

Women, even though your master does not tell you to ask a blessing from God, I'm telling you to. If there were no God, there would be no human life, that's how it is!

That's it, go ahead!

Sangut's role as virtual spokesman for the good on the side of the villain is evident. Here the *panasar* speaks with considerable authority, but it is as a court servant of high rank rather than as a divinity in his own right that he does so.

13

Comic dancing is a staple ingredient of South Balinese shadowplay. Delem and Tualen dance in nearly every performance, and Sangut and Mredah often join in as well. These dances are executed somewhat differently by different puppeteers. Like many other elements in the show they are modular units that may be inserted at an appropriate time. Internally they are further divisible into smaller component modules which may be varied and rearranged within the larger structures determined by the music. Great variety is made possible by simple recombination of the stock phrases. Subject always to constraints imposed by the unalterable character traits of the dancers, the comic dance routines are subject to a considerable amount of variation from one performance to the next, tailored not so much to the circumstances of the plot as to the *dalang*'s exuberance (or lack of it) on the occasion. Each dance reveals the dancing puppet's character in essence. As a dancer, Delem is chesty, arrogant, pompous and silly; he moves like a demented fighting cock.

(DELEM *enters, very excited. The musicians play "Delem's Song", and he begins to dance with wild abandon. Between flurries of dancing he pauses and sings a pious and learned quotation from the classics.*)
DELEM: *So this is the propitious plan.*
If he can kill that enemy, and become wise,
In order to ascend to excellence and well-being...
Not lower than Indra's heaven will he attain.
(*He dances with wild abandon.* SANGUT *observes him. Audience applause.*)
Sangut!
SANGUT: Hey!
DELEM: Look there!
    (SANGUT *looks off screen to the right.*)
SANGUT: Yes?
DELEM: How many monkeys are there, Sangut?
SANGUT: What do you want them for?
DELEM: Eat 'em. Roast the monkeys, Sangut! They'll taste delicious.
    Yum! (*Audience laughter.*)
    (DELEM *dances faster and faster.*
SANGUT: What are you doing? You're going so fast I'm seeing stars.
    You'll trample on your own feet! Oh oh!
    (DELEM *dances wildly and swings his arms, out of control.*)
    Stop now. Stop! Sit down, Delem. Don't jump up and down like
    that! Hey!
    (DELEM *finally stops dancing. The music also stops.*)

14

In addition to quick gags and jokes, the *panasar* may take part in elaborate and extended comic routines that are set up, structured and timed with fastidious craftsmanship, as in the following example. Sangut has been providing exposition as he warns Delem of the powerful strength of their enemy, the Monkey King Sugriwa. But the puppeteer develops the sequence into a major joke, one producing a laugh big enough to serve as a climax and conclusion for the first act of the play.

SANGUT: Lord, those monkeys! They aren't messing around, Why, I remember the head of the monkeys, Sugriwa. Wow! High rank, that one.

When he fought with Prime Minister Dumeraksa in the past, how they rolled and tumbled! Every time he bit him he pinched him. That ogre was as big as a cockfight arena and he got his guts ripped out just like that. His guts were plucked out and scattered, "Pow!"—just like that! (*Audience laughter.*)

If Lord Sugriwa strikes an enemy with a blow, Wham! He doesn't need a second one. Smash! The victim doesn't even get to ask for water Lordy! If he hits a mountain, it splits!

(*He demonstrates a "one-two" punch.*)

DELEM: Bah! The way you act!

SANGUT: Don't mess around, Delem. When he was fighting with Lord Dumeraksa, you know what happened? Why, he picked up a tree, Sugriwa did, just plucked it right up. What did he use, would you say? What kind of tree would you say he chose? Some shrub? Its trunk was surely a hundred yards around. When it was pulled up, "Poof!" the whole country went dark. When he stripped off the twigs, it was like a dust storm hit the country, Lord. That's what Sugriwa used to hit him with, but nothing happened. After that blow I thought he had come for nothing. But "Bam!"—just like that he pulled up the mountain, why he carried the mountain. How strong, Lordy! Wow! How he could hit!

(DELEM *is fascinated.*)

Practice was the reason he was able to do it. From the time when he was little, as soon as he was able to think, as soon as he was able to walk, he started to practice boxing. If he practiced kicking, well, he did it until he could kick higher than his head. His hands were really tough. He struck without thinking about his fingers. They were swollen, swollen, just like...like...like your goitre, Delem! (*He points at DELEM's goitre. Audience laughter.*)

Man! How he practiced, isn't that so, Delem? In his front yard there
was a tree, a big tree. He hung up a big sack filled with little
bits of coral. Coral and sand. When he went out to get food, he'd
go into the yard and "Sock! Pow! Wham! Bam!"
(*He demonstrates a series of blows.*)
And then he'd go out. Later, he'd come home after going for a
walk. "Wham, wham!" He'd hit it again when he came home.
Then he'd practice to toughen up his feet, the same way. he'd go
out in the morning. "Wham, wham!" Make the left hand tough,
"Wham, wham, wham, wham!!!"
(*His demonstration picks up speed until he suddenly begins to beat*
DELEM *mercilessly. As the audience cheers and applauds,* DELEM
recovers and chases SANGUT *off the screen.*)"

It has often been observed that comedy is regenerative in nature. Like
the Wily Coyote in a children's film cartoon, who pops up unscathed
at once after being flattened by a steam roller, Delem recovers instantly
and completely from the beating he receives from Sangut. As in the
West, much Balinese humor is a matter of very abrupt changes of tone
and intention: Delem is beaten, yowls with pain, recovers, sees Sangut,
he yells, Sangut runs, Delem chases him with arms rotating like a
windmill—all in a very few seconds. The puppeteer, a master of his
craft, carefully builds a clear and coherent sequence of visual impressions.
He thus creates a linked chain of comedic stimuli and responses that
build to an uproarious climax.

15

(TUALEN *enters, dancing with comic awkwardness.*)
TUALEN: (*Singing as he dances*) *Thus admonished was his younger*
    brother, 'I [your older brother] am happy and clear in mind.'
(*He dances stiffly and ponderously, to 'Tualen's Song'.*)
At dawn of day the Pandawas rose,
Marching forth from Wirata city.
(Mredah *enters and watches his father dance.* TUALEN *gets excited and*
    drags his son into it.
MREDAH: Hey, you're pulling my nose! (*Audience laughter.*)
TUALEN: Don't be foolish. Behave yourself back there!
(*With* MREDAH *behind him,* TUALEN *dances more vigorously.*)
Not different were they from the sun,
Rising o'er the Eastern peaks.
(*He goes on dancing, concluding each phrase of music by bopping*
    MREDAH *on the top of the head with his fist. Audience laughter.*)

MREDAH: You're using my head for a gong! (*Audience laughter.*) (TUALEN *concludes his dance and "Tualen's Song" comes to an end. He is huffing and puffing from the exertion.*)

Tualen's dancing is slow and reflects his character. The audience registers continuous amusement as he dances. His son, Mredah, is an intrinsic part of the act, serving as a kind of interlocutor and straightman. By registering big "takes," he coaches the audience to laugh at old Tualen, who is here functioning as clown.

Much of the humor in Tualen's dance arises from tight and well-rehearsed coordination with the accompanying musical ensemble. Toward the end of the dance, when the music has proceeded to its fastest section, he gets a series of laughs by repeatedly striking Mredah on the head exactly on the stroke of the gong tones which punctuate each musical phrase; the joke depends on his achieving a sudden coincidence of gesture and the musical sound. Such intentional coincidences are common in Balinese classical dancing[5] as well as in comedy.

16

Comic song in Balinese theater is a large and complex topic requiring separate investigation. All the genres of popular theater, such as *wayang kulit, arja, drama gong, topeng prembon* are very rich in comic singing. The play under consideration here does not, however, contain many examples. Delem's song (see above) is an integral part of his dance, giving further illustration of his brash and forward personality through the manner of his vocalizing.

In another example, Tualen gets laughter by singing, unaccompanied, a garbled quotation from one or another of the Balinese literary classics. The humor derives entirely from his quavering, off-pitch delivery. The text bears no relationship to the situation.

TUALEN: Well, sit down for a moment so we can rest, Mredah! Wow!
(*Singing*) *Without being pushed away, he put aside, ide, ide, ide. What was in order, er, er, er.*
Especially that which he would swing away, ay, ay, ay.
Destroy, oy, oy, oyed! (*Audience laughter.*)
MREDAH: (*Bursts out*) Your tongue is stiff, that's it! You're old, don't carry on! What are you doing?
(MREDAH *slaps* TUALEN *on the back, Audience laughter.*)

The main purpose of the song, however, is to serve as a bridge into one of the major didactic passages of the play, an extended disquisition on the subject of proper respect for the elderly. By drawing the audience into laughing at Tualen, Mredah makes them complicit and thus deepens the bite of the homily that is about to be delivered.

TUALEN: Well! What are you saying Mredah? My tongue is stiff, is that it? Go ahead! If your daddy is old now he has a lot of defects: stiff tongue, teeth gone, eyes dim, ears deaf. That's how it is with someone who is old, so you'll know. But daddy was once a young bachelor like you.

When I was a youth like you, I had a lot of sharp teeth, sharp ears, keen eyes. I was clever at speaking. Hah! I was more clever at speaking than you are when I was still a youth. Because your daddy is already old now, already weak, all my apparatus is inadequate. That's why I'm confused. So don't be so quick to criticize your daddy's age.

The lesson continues at some length. To make his points lively and clear, Tualen develops his theme with images drawn from village life, just as Sangut has done earlier in the play:

TUALEN: Yep, when you were just born, you didn't have a single tooth. I had to chew your rice for you and feed it to you bit by bit, into your mouth here. So that you would grow up quickly. When you were old enough to know East from West, I put thoughts into you. If I had two cents' worth of intelligence, I put it into your belly, so that you would get smart. But once you got smart, your daddy was stupid!

It's like, for example, boiling coconut milk to get the oil. If I get a cupful, you take a cupful. Daddy is old now and just has the coconut milk without any oil, and the dry gratings. That was so you would be smart.

The real reason I'm old is you! If it weren't for you I wouldn't be old. Lordy! So go slow. Why, if you just think about it, papa faces the same dangers you do; we're both equally human, you and I.

Even though you have many sharp teeth now, later on you'll be toothless like me. As clever as you are now, you'll just be old later on—confused, deaf, half blind, yep, that's how it will be."

At the end of the sequence, Mredah, still the straightman, concedes: "Yes, now I know. Yep, if that's how it is, from now on I won't be fresh to old people."[6]

It has frequently been observed that Balinese religion is based on orthopraxis or common worship rather than on orthodoxy or common belief, and that formal ceremonials in Balinese religion are focussed on the performance of ritual acts rather than on pious exhortation. Balinese priests do not give sermons or teach public lessons as part of their normal office. The role of teacher and preacher was formerly reserved for the *topeng pajegan* dancer[7] and the *dalang*. The *panasar* are clearly the most appropriate characters to exercise this instructive function in *wayang*, especially Sangut, the skeptic, on the left and Tualen, the paternal authority, on the right.

The didactic possibilities of the medium have been recognized by the Indonesian government and by local authorities, who encourage the puppeteers to include authorized government messages on such topics as birth control, proper diet, etc. in each performance. None, however, was included on this occasion.[8]

17
Tualen ends the lesson on aging with a mildly bawdy joke:

TUALEN: (*Joking*) Can you imagine? I got in a great sweat that time when I made you! (*Audience laughter.*)
MREDAH: What is he saying? (*Audience laughter.*)

Here again a secondary laugh is achieved by Mredah as a result of a well-timed reaction. The sequence is familiar to comedians in many traditions: stimulus, comic "take", pause, reply, laugh.

Humor involving sexuality is an indispensable resource of the Balinese puppeteer, but it is not a prominent element here. "The Death of Kumbakarna" contains a minimum of such material, as the source does not offer many possibilities along these lines. Plays with plots centered on romance and courtship provide greater scope for good-natured, mildly off-color clowning by the servants.

18
Balinese comedy often involves play with fear and startling. This unsophisticated little passage, which is part of an accelerating series of jokes and little sight-gags, might have been part of a Three Stooges routine:

(TUALEN *is calling the* MONKEYS.)

MREDAH: (*Sneaking up from behind*) Hoot! Hoot! Hoot!
(TUALEN *jumps, surprised. Audience laughter.*)
TUALEN: Calm down! You'll scare the wind out of me! (*Audience laughter.*)

19

The next example demonstrates a well-planned joke that depends to a great extent on the timing of the anticlimactic punchline. The pause sets up an inflated expectation, the punchline sets off the laughter, and then Tualen helps the laugh along with his carefully placed "That's it!)

TUALEN: (*calls again.*) HEY! COME OUT! COME HERE!
MONKEYS: (*From off screen*) SQUAWWWK!
TUALEN: What's that?
(*Several small monkeys rush in and jump about, frolicking and playing. Squawking loudly, they tease and pester* TUALEN.)
      Hey, Get down! Get down!
(*The monkeys continue to tease him.*)
   Quiet! Is it right for you to bother with me? Is it right? It's not right! You little guys are screaming.
   Even though you are in the form of monkeys, if you behave yourselves now while you're monkeys, later on if you're lucky, in another incarnation, you might become, become,...Apes! That's it! (*Audience laughter.*)

20

During the section of the play called the Departure (*Pangkat*), in which the monkey army departs for the field, short comic routines are interspersed among the passages devoted to exciting pre-battle action to lend variety and a measure of comic relief.

(TUALEN *looks off screen and sees a small* MONKEY *with a watermelon.*)
TUALEN: Hey you! Where did you get the watermelon?
MONKEY: Squawk!
TUALEN: Go look for one for me!
MONKEY: Squawk! (*The* MONKEY *runs away.* TUALEN *shakes his fist. Audience laughter.*)
(*A mischievous monkey rushes out and grabs* TUALEN *below the belt.*)
TUALEN: Hey! Damn you! Here's a naughty monkey!
MREDAH: What is it, Dad? How are you?
TUALEN: He grabbed my ignition key! Phew! (*Audience laughter.*)

Here Tualen interweaves contemporary elements into the ancient time frame of the old epic source and draws humor from the shift of context. His attitude is good-natured and avuncular rather than angry.

Another example of comic byplay:

(*Several small* MONKEYS *cross the screen. They are also hurrying to the battle front. Then a single small* MONKEY *crosses; his private parts, clearly visible, are wagging back and forth. Audience laughter.*)

TUALEN: His bicycle stand keeps slipping down! (*Audience laughter.*)

Tualen extends the impact of this classic "sight gag" by "pointing" it with a witty remark that serves as a caption.

22

The Departure sequence features repeated bits of action, in which several of the monkey leaders dance, pull up trees by the roots, and strut their prowess. Comedy and action alternate in quick succession.

(MONKEYS *cross the screen in great numbers. The musicians change to "Nala", and* NALA *and* NILA *come in, leaping about and throwing rocks.*)

NALA and NILA: Squawk! Squawk!

(NILA *exits.* NALA *dances and pulls up trees and hurls trees and rocks off left at the enemy. He exits.*

TUALEN *enters, from left. Flying rocks sail over his head, then one strikes him. He rushes off right to get his shield, returns and throws it off left. He exits, chasing his shield.* MREDAH *enters. The shield flies on to the screen from the right and strikes him on the head. Audience laughter.*)

MREDAH: Hey! (*He runs off in pursuit.*)

(MREDAH *rushes up to* TUALEN *to confront him about the shield.* TUALEN *breaks wind in* MREDAH's *face, and sends him reeling backward. Audience laughter.*)

Oh me! (*Audience laughter.*)

Here the "snapper" (the part of a joke that actually triggers the laugh) is the *dalang*'s exquisite vocal fart imitation, but the audience response reaches its peak with Mredah's staggering reaction. As several of the contributors to this volume attest, comic flatulence is a very important resource of traditional puppeteers all over the world.

23

(TUALEN *approaches a tree, intending to use it as a weapon.*)

TUALEN: Yep, a tree! I'm going to fight too. I don't just need your fruit. I'm going to use you as a weapon because of the curse of Lady Jambi long ago. They say you are a reincarnation of Lady Jambi and are supposed to be used as weapons by the monkey nation.

(*He gives the tree a mighty tug, but he cannot move it.*)

Well! You won't give yourself to be used as a weapon! Be careful or I'll eat you up myself. Oooh!

(*He tries again. This time the tree comes up easily, falling on him and pinning him beneath its branches.* MREDAH *returns and finds him trapped there.*)

MREDAH: Good Lord, Daddy! Oh, Dad, Dad, Dad.

TUALEN: How delightful to taste all kinds of fruits!

(*Pretending to be completely unconcerned by his predicament,* TUALEN sings phrases from a Javanese song.)

They are all students,
Encircling the teak tree
While the moon is clear.

Who's that?

MREDAH: Wow, Daddy! A tree is crushing you.

TUALEN: What's up, Mredah? Can't you pull me out?

MREDAH: Nope.

TUALEN: Why not? Too heavy?

MREDAH: Okay, Dad. Lift together, Dad. Quickly, Dad!

(*They struggle to lift the tree off, in vain.* MREDAH *climbs into the tree that is trapping* TUALEN *and begins to eat the fruit he finds there. Audience laughter.*)

TUALEN: You're too stingy. Be more humane! So now you're clever at climbing. Throw down one of those rotten fruits to Daddy. You're filling up your belly all by yourself.

MREDAH *comes down, and again they try to pull* TUALEN *out from under the tree that is weighing down on him.*)

MREDAH: Yeah, yeah, Dad, lift it quickly.

(*They struggle with the tree.*)

TUALEN: Stop! Wait! Wow!

MREDAH: What is it, Daddy?

(TUALEN *does not respond.*)

Just do what I'm doing, like this!

(*No response.*)

What do you say, Dad?

(*No response.*)

Daddy's very dizzy!

TUALEN: (*Full of self pity*) Why I've been thrown away. Just leave me behind now, just leave me behind!

MREDAH: Let's just pull together, how about it?

(*They struggle with the tree again.*)

TUALEN: All together, Mredah! Unh!

(*Successful at last they throw off the tree. Audience applause.*)

It is the situation that is comic in the preceding example: Tualen experiences an amusing reversal as a result of trying to imitate his powerful masters. The premise would have been familiar to an Elizabethan playwright. In contrast with some of the previously cited examples, this section does not lead up to a climatic joke.

24

(*Many* MONKEYS *cross the screen.* SUGRIWA *reappears, throwing rocks. He comes upon* TUALEN *and seizes him from behind.*)

SUGRIWA: Squawk!

TUALEN: You've caught me, sir!

SUGRIWA: I thought you were a stone!

TUALEN: Thought I was a stone?

SUGRIWA: Indeed! (*Audience laughter.*)

(SUGRIWA *throws him down and exits.* MREDAH *enters.*)

TUALEN: Poor me!

MREDAH: What's the matter, Daddy?

TUALEN: When I came up behind him, he caught me. 'Why did you grab me?' I asked him. 'Thought you were a rock,' [he said]. That's what!

MREDAH: Your body is black, like a rock, that's it. You better get away. He uses rocks for weapons as well as trees.

TUALEN: (*Offended*) And you look like you were just polished with coconut cream! (*Audience laughter.*)

MREDAH: Oh, Daddy!

At the very end of the play, Tualen completes the tale by providing the denouement:

(RAMA *shoots* KUMBAKARNA *with a magic arrow. He dies.*)

TUALEN: He was brave in defense of Alengka, and he will find heaven. (*To the body of* KUMBAKARNA) He, Lord Rama, avatar of the God Wisnu, will exorcise the monstrous qualities form your nature, for you succeeded in becoming a true and virtuous exponent of the Law.

(*The* kakayonan *is planted center screen, indicating that the performance has come to an end.*)[9]

***

It is clear from the examples given above that each of the *panasar* must be a formidably talented entertainer, with a broad spectrum of theatrical skills; even more gifted, than, is the *dalang* who must bring all four of them to life, in addition to a host of other characters. Not only do the *panasar* contribute essentially to shaping the most basic structures and dramaturgical units of the play, they broaden the range of available expression across a spectrum of utterance and behavior that ranges from the merely lively or vivid all the way to routines provoking outbursts of laughter and applause from the spectators. From the standpoint of technique, we see highly-polished, well-rehearsed sketches and routines that would be a credit to professional humorists or comedians anywhere in the world. In the hands of a skillful Balinese *dalang*, the technique and the material are at an equally high level.

The *panasar* also play an important part in conveying the intellectual and ideological content of the play to the audience. They serve both to preserve and reinvigorate the traditional codes of conduct and language, for even as they test the barriers of conventionally acceptable behavior they bring the relevant codes into focus, foregrounding the traditional social order and, on balance, reaffirming it.

Notes

[1]Relevant sources include Frederik E. deBoer, "Pak Rajeg's life in art; [biography of a Balinese dalang]," *TDR* 23/2 (number T82) (1979), pp. 57-62; Frederik E. deBoer, "The *Dimba and Dimbi* of I Nyoman Rajeg; a Balinese Shadow Play," *Asian Theatre Journal* 4/1 (Spring, 1987), pp. 76-107; "*The Death of Kumbakarna* of I Ketut Madra; a Balinese *Wayang Ramayana* Play" (in preparation); Leland W. Gralapp, "Balinese painting and the Wayang tradition," *Artibus Asia* 29 (1967), pp. 239-266; H.I.R. Hinzler, *Bima Swarga in Balinese Wayang*. Verhandelingen van het Koninklijk Instituut voor Taal-,Land- en Volkenkunde 90 (The Hague: Martinus Nijhoff, 1981); Angela Hobart, "Notes on the making of Balinese Shadow Puppets," *Art and Archaelogy Research Papers* 10 (December, 1976), pp. 40-47; Angela Hobart, "Between things: the place of the *Pendasar* in Bali," *Archipel* 25 (1983), pp. xx-xx; Angela Hobart, "The Kakayonan: the Cosmic Tree or World Mountain," *Indonesia Circle* 30 (March, 1983), pp. 13-16; C. Hooykaas, "The function of the dalang," in *Akten des XXIX Internationalen Orientalisten Kongresses, Muenchen, 1957* (1957), pp. 683-686; C. Hooykaas, "Two Exorcist Priests from Bali," *Man* 60 (December, 1960), pp. 180-181; C. Hooykaas, *Kama and Kala: Materials for the study of the Shadow Theatre in Bali*. Verhandelingen der Nederlandse Akademie van Wetenschapen, afd.

Letterkunde: New series, pt. 79. (Amsterdam & London: North Holland Publishing Co., 1973); Colin McPhee, "The Balinese Wayang Koelit and its Music," *Djawa* 16 (1936) pp. 1-34; Larry Reed, "Bima Swarga: a Balinese Shadow Play as performed by Ida Bagus Ngurah [Buduk]," *Asian Theatre Journal* 3/1 (Spring, 1986), pp. 1-33; I Nyoman Sumandhi, "Wayang Calonarang," unpublished MA thesis, Wesleyan University; and Mary Zurbuchen, *The Shadow Theater of Bali: Explorations in language and text.* (Princeton: Princeton University Press 1987).

[2]A complete text and translation of this performance, along with commentary and a biography of the *dalang*, is currently nearing completion (deBoer, in preparation). I Ketut Madra died, tragically young, in a traffic accident in 1979.

[3]The story goes that when the Hindu pantheon first arrived on Bali from Java these old, indigenous deities chose to remain on earth to serve, advise and be companions to the newer "generation" of gods, demigods, heroes, villains and ogres rather than retire to their places in heaven.

[4]Differences exist among the various regions of Bali with respect to the presence or absence of different (in North Bali) or additional (North Bali, Tabanan) *panasar*. However, in Badung and Gianyar, the South Balinese "heartland," only Tualen, Mredah, Sangut, and Delem typically appear. Condong, the maidservant, who attends women and children, has many functions in common with the *panasar*, but she is the proper subject for a separate article.

[5]See I Madé Bandem and Fredrik E. deBoer, *Kaja and Kelod: Balinese Dance in Transition* (Kuala Lumpur: Oxford University Press, 1981), pp. 82, 85, 86.

[6]This lengthy setpiece was a favorite of *dalang* Madra, who included it in very much the same form in many different plays. It appears, for example, in the Kawi/Balinese text of his play "Kuntiyadnya" (I Ketut Madra, "Kuntiyadnya," in *Pakem Wayang Parwa Bali* [Denpasar, Bali, Indonesia: Yayasan Pewayangan Daerah Bali, 1978], pp. 32-34) as well as in unpublished performance transcriptions in the author's collection.

[7]See Bandem and deBoer, pp. 51-61.

[8]Although perhaps the reference to "eating to live" made by Sangut above (p. xxx) represents a vestigial remnant of such a communication.

[9] Hinzler, pp. 165-167, describes the use of the *panasar* and especially Tualen in the *dalang*'s post-production ritual. During this part of the performance, which is not seen by the audience, Tualen speaks the *mantra* and performs the gestures which consecrate the offerings.

The Form and Function of Humor in the Liège Puppet Theater

Joan E. Gross

Introduction

Humor in the Liège puppet theater, like humor elsewhere, is based on relationships of incongruity. Three kinds of incongruity are apparent in this tradition, though they often overlap. First of all, there is the incongruity of imagery, when images which generally occur in separate realms are welded into a single image. This usually involves the degradation of that which is lofty and abstract into that which pertains to the body and material living. Exaggeration is the second general area of incongruity. This covers characterization, whether in the physical construction of the puppet or in the linguistic construction of the way the character speaks. Lastly, there is the area of frame-breaking,[1] which is an area in which the puppet theater excels since it is separated from other human experiences by frames and uses frames in ways different from both human interaction and live theater. Since frames act as interpretive tools, the breaking of a frame results in a moment of confusion which can often be humorous. Incongruous elements pervade all aspects of the Liège puppet show, so the following discussion is organized according to the separate aspects of the live performance[2] in which the various types of humor outlined above can be seen. It is hoped that this arrangement will allow for easier comparison with the work of those who are operating under different theoretical frameworks. The aspects of the performance which will be explored for their humorous content are: nonlinguistic, nonsegmental linguistic, accent, dialect, word play, framing, and genre. In the section on word play, both the formal linguistic manipulations and the imagery, rich in references to the oral, anal, and sexual, are examined.

While this paper concentrates on the form of humor in the puppet theater, in the conclusion some of the functions humor fulfills are commented upon. One of its functions is to stand in opposition to the official culture, embodied in the standard language and rules of politeness. With this in mind, it is imperative to point out that it is the commoner characters, or tchantchès, who are the agents of the humor, in contrast

106

to the upper class characters who are all quite serious. In fact, I suggest that within Liège puppet shows, humor is a "way of speaking" specific to the lower class.[3] Before launching into this discussion of humor in the Liège puppet theater, a few words must be said about the nature of the theater, the chief comic character (Tchantchès), and some of the animators of this theater.

Performers, Wooden and Human

Liège, the cultural capital of French speaking Belgium, has long been known for the puppetry tradition practiced there since the mid-nineteenth century. The puppets, which may stand up to a meter tall, are carved out of wood with articulations at the neck, shoulders, hips and knees. However, the only instrument of direct control is a single steel rod which is attached to a ring at the top of the head. This means that the puppets move in a very stiff, un-humanlike manner. Many of the plays they perform are based on medieval chivalric epics, although later material is also used.

One cannot embark on a discussion of comedy in the Liège puppet theater without first introducing Tchantchès, the commoner hero of Liège. Tchantchès is the cousin of Kasperl, Gianduja, Guignol, Woltje and other regional comic characters all over the world who find themselves in the puppet theater. Like most of his cousins, he speaks directly to the audience in the language of the common man. He stands shorter than the noble characters who share the stage with him and can also be distinguished from them by his costume which consists of a navy blue smock and cap, a red neckerchief and wooden shoes, the costume worn by nineteenth-century workers and peasants in Belgium. Tchantchès' class membership is established linguistically as well as visually, as he pronounces colorful expressions in a mixture of French and Walloon, the regional Gallo-Romance dialect. He has not been to school and therefore confuses "right" and "left" and cannot count but he is known for his native intelligence which enables him to fight for good and against evil. Of course, he could not do this without his keen fighting ability. Using only his feet and his head, Tchantchès destroys all his adversaries who sport mighty weapons and solid armor or possess magical powers. Tchantchès does not take life too seriously though, and prefers to spend his time drinking "pèkèt" (the local eau de vie or schnapps) with his friends, much to the dismay of his mate, Nanesse. No situation is so grave that Tchantchès cannot step back and poke fun at it and, while he may act as the mere servant to Charlemagne, Tchantchès is the real hero of the puppet show and elicits raucous cheering and shrieks of laughter from the audience.

Belgian puppets Roland, Tchantchès and Nanesse. Photo: A. Pasqualino

Behind this puppet form stands a human who identifies very closely with this character, even to the extent of answering to the name of Tchantchès. He is the master puppeteer who has created Tchantchès in his own image. This man also creates every other puppet character on stage by means of style and voice manipulation. In a sense these characters can all be seen as parts of the puppeteer's self, since everyone has multiple images of themselves. However, Tchantchès is special, for he stands in for the puppeteer on stage. When the puppeteer wants to convey something directly to the audience, he generally says it through the mouth of Tchantchès.[4] In fact, Tchantchès is of such importance that his name is used to refer to the entire group of commoner characters which appear in Liège puppet shows. The individual puppet introduced above is the most important character in this group or, in other words, Tchantchès is the most important tchantchès, but all the tchantchès can be (and usually are) funny. It is through this group of characters that the puppeteer plies his humorous wares.

Humor is an important part of the resources of every puppeteer in Liège, though each one may use it in a different manner, depending partly on his training and the audience for whom he generally performs. For instance, the puppeteers who did not train for long periods of time under an older puppeteer use less traditional folk humor and slapstick gags and more contemporary humor, employing irony and satire. They are also more successful among adult spectators. In light of these differences, it is necessary to recognize the individual performers in this paper. Names are only omitted when referring to a gag or phrase used by several puppeteers. The four puppeteers from whom examples are drawn throughout this paper are: Adrien Dufour, Henri Libert, Jean Pinet, and Christian Deville.

Adrien Dufour was born in 1909 to a coal miner father and a mother who worked in a textile factory in Liège. By the time he was nine years old, he was helping out in two puppet theaters, one belonging to his uncle. By age twenty-five, he was performing regularly at the Museum of Walloon Life where he still performs. His audience consists mostly of children, not uncommonly brought by their grandparents. The class composition appears to be mostly bourgeois and there are occasionally non-liégeois groups who visit the museum.

Henri Libert, son of a printing press worker, did not have any other puppeteers in his family nor did he work as an assistant to an older puppeteer. He did, however, become interested in puppetry at a young age and by the time he was twelve, he was performing puppet shows for his friends in his native village of Nessanvaux, about 15 km east of Liège. In his mid twenties, soon after World War II, he put a theater together and began performing at various carnivals and celebrations around Liège, between stints at his permanent job of house painting. He gained quite a reputation and eventually was approached to perform weekly in the Tchantchès Museum of Outre Meuse. The audience is mainly bourgeois and a mixture of both parents and children.

Jean Pinet, a shop teacher in his early forties, claims to be the fifth generation of puppeteers in his family. He performs at the Museum of Walloon Life on occasion, but he also has an itinerant theater. Half of the traveling shows he presents in schools and, of the other half, 65% to 70% are also for children. The class background of his audience is varied.

Christian Deville is carrying on the fair tradition of Liégeois marionettes started by Gaston Engels in 1927. Deville began helping out Engels (an outstanding showman from a long line of puppeteers) in the early 1950s when he was nine years old. He worked in a café at night and in a steel mill during the day in order to get the money together to buy a set of puppets from Engels. He refused to perform until Engels made him a Tchantchès exactly like his own. Now, Deville works on the road crew of the city of Liège and performs on weekends at various festivals around the city. His audience consists of children who are largely of working class background.

Nonlinguistic Humor

The nonlinguistic comic element most evident in the Liège puppet theater is the physical appearance of some of the puppets. While the noble characters are intricately carved to be quite handsome and serious and the evil magical characters often are quite frightening, the more common characters, both peasant/workers and the few bourgeois personages, often possess disproportionately large heads, gaping mouths, gigantic noses and ill-fitting clothes. More than one puppeteer has told me that many of these characters were originally carved to be caricatures of well-known people in the neighborhood, but nowadays when new ones are carved, puppets, rather than people, serve as the models. However, contemporary personages can occasionally be linked to one of these older puppets. In his nativity play, for example, Libert used one of these puppets to represent the present day prime minister. The audience laughed heartily to see the disproportionate features of this puppet/prime minister. The fact that they had seen this puppet in other roles made it all the more hilarious because the prime minister could be linked with the other characters played by this puppet. In this same scene, Tchantchès announced the arrival of his nephew, Hubert, the university student. The puppet that emerged had a head ten times the size of any other puppet on stage. The term "Grosse tête" which refers to an important person who generally has a good education, also carries with it a sense of arrogance and vanity. These latter qualities were aptly portrayed by Hubert who proceeded to quote article, page, chapter, paragraph, and line of the charter for the Association of Intellectual Liégeois. In this case, a metaphor was literally carved into a ridiculous character.

The liégeois puppets are rather restricted in movement having only a single rod through their heads for manipulation purposes. However, only an uninitiated spectator would view their stiff movements as being comic because this is simply how the puppets move. The only movement which is thought extremely funny by the young children is when Tchantchès trips or runs into the wall when leaving the stage. This can be performed several times during a show and never loses its comic effect among the younger members of the audience who are the biggest fans of this kind of slapstick humor. Occasionally there are other puppet actions which are funny, but the comic effect stems from the linguistic accompaniment rather than the physical manifestation alone. This is the case for instance, when a soldier is gagged by the Saracens in Libert's theater and returns to his camp with his hands tied behind him. His sergeant asks him to explain what happened and the soldier starts excitedly mumbling under his gag. The sergeant then turns to the audience and says "His pronunciation isn't very good." Here we have a linguistic remark which depends on a visual counterpart for its humor and vice versa. The gagged puppet is not funny without the mumbling and the humor is highlighted by the sergeant's ironic comment. The incongruity of asking someone to explain something with a gag in his mouth would be comical even in the live theater. In the puppet theater, however, there is another level of incongruity because the puppet's mouth is not the site of language. The audience is led to misframe the puppet as a live, speaking person since it can see that a physical alteration to the puppet's mouth changes the quality of the voice. Perhaps they laugh when they realize that they have been fooled.

The Voice

Most of the comedy in the Liège puppet theater is vocal in nature. First of all, in the realm of nonsegmentals, several voice qualities that the puppeteers use for their tchantchès are inherently funny. These are not used for Tchantchès himself, but for his friends.[5] Among the most common are a high pitched, strident, nasalized voice; a slobbery voice, produced by pressing the sides of the cheeks against the teeth and forcing all palatal sounds through an abundance of saliva; and a low muffled sepulchral voice with nasalization. Stuttering is a voice qualification that is considered humorous. Sometimes it will mark the normal way of speaking for certain tchantchès, but it is often used for non-stuttering characters to signify that they are scared.

The voice is used in other ways as well to produce a comic effect. Loud snoring and uncontrolled laughter are the most common of these. The uncontrolled laughter with which the puppet Pierre Long Nez begins Deville's shows is identical to that of Deville's teacher, Gaston Engels, indicating that these vocal dramatizations are important resources to a puppeteer, and successful ones are imitated. Another puppeteer told me that he learned how to snore (a long implosive uvular fricative followed by a whistle) by listening to a Karagöz tape which he bought in a store which catered to Turkish immigrants in Liège.

Accents

The use of different accents is another way in which puppeteers differentiate characters in a humorous way. The most common non-native accent that Liège puppeteers imitate is that of a Fleming. This character is a tchantchès figure, so his Flemish accent is mapped onto a mixture of French and Walloon, the language of all the tchantchès. His speech is clipped and sometimes sing-songy and "te" is used instead of "tu" and is inserted in various other places. He may also throw in occasional common Flemish words like "meneer" and "Godverdome." Libert is a master of such accents. Besides the Flemish tchantchès, he has one from Verviers (a city to the east of Liège) who draws out his vowels and has a very peculiar intonation pattern, as well as one from the Ardennes who speaks with an apical trilled /r/. The uvular /R/ became a marker of prestige in the 17th century and spread from Paris to other urban centers and outwards from each one of these centers.[6] It appears to have been present in Liège for quite some time as even the Walloon of Liège is said to have always had the uvular /R/. The apical /r/ is seen as being more countrified, which it is in a sense since the areas farthest away from urban centers have retained it. The Ardennes, the domain of hills and forests to the south of Liège, is one such area. Libert may also use the apical /r/ to mark the accents common to Italian and Arab guest-workers, but these characters speak French and not a French/Walloon mixture.

Use of the Regional Dialect

The humor of these nonsegmental manipulations and accents in the puppet theater lies in that they are all caricatures: certain features are exaggerated and others are ignored. The association of Walloon and humor has a different source. It stems from the fact that the non-standard dialect is opposed to the standard language in the same way that comedy is opposed to that which is official and serious. This is why we see such widespread use of non-standard dialects for comic purposes around the world. This is especially evident in the puppet theater where it is often the case that comic characters speak in dialect while the others speak the standard language.[7] The opposition of comedy to official or "high" culture is also the reason comedy is so often associated with the lower class, who, in addition, are the people who still speak non-standard regional dialects. The crude, yet colorful images evoked by the regional dialect make it a perfect instrument for comedy. I have seen more than one popular Liège cabaret variety show in which all the acts were in French except for the comedians who performed at least half their material in Walloon, usually the half which contained the jokes' punch lines. (This should ring familiar to those readers who have heard jokes by older American Jews who use Yiddish in the same way.) As for Walloon theaters, of which there are two which perform regularly in Liège, most of the plays, and for certain the most successful ones, are comedies. One of these, *Tatî l' Pèriquî* about a simple barber who thinks he has won the lottery and begins putting on airs, is performed in the puppet theater on occasion.

Adults who know some Walloon find the colorful images created in this language very amusing. Children who do not know Walloon sometimes conjure up a funnier referent to Walloon words than those who do know the language. For instance, the word for young girl in Walloon is "crapode," which usually elicits giggles from the audience when used in a puppet show. The children, however, do not know that it means "young girl." Instead, they make the analogy to the closest French word they know which is "crapaud", meaning "toad", and are quite amused that puppets go around calling girls toads.

Word Play: Poetics, Puns, Hyperbole, and Degradation

Certain Walloon sounds which do not occur in French, for instance the /c/, which occurs twice in "Tchantchès", are considered amusing by children even if they do not know the meaning of the word. Sounds do not have to be strange in and of themselves if they are combined in interesting manners. Children are very sensitive to the arrangement of sounds whether into real words or nonsense words. One such word that the puppeteers use is "scoubidou" which is a name they call witches and other disreputable sorts. The children laugh whenever they hear this word which nicely contrasts high back rounded vowels with a high front unrounded one. Puppeteers use rhyme, alliteration, and other forms of parallelism to increase the focus on the form of the language. Hyperbole and bodily allusions create humorous representations in the minds of the listeners. Below, the reader will find two excerpts which show some of the different poetic techniques used in the puppet theater. The first excerpt was spoken by Deville's Tchantchès to a predominantly child audience. The second was said by a knight in Libert's theater in front of a mixed (child/adult) audience. However, only the adults laughed.

1. TCHANTCHES: Et plus vite que tout de suite encore, tu vas ramasser mes quarante-huit coups de pieds dans ton panê-cou et je vais t'envoyer dans la caisse aux cliquottes.
2. CHARLEMAGNE: Et que vas-tu faire pendant cette retraite?
    KNIGHT: Seigneur, je vais faire comme d'habitude ce que vous me direz de faire seigneur en faisant tout mon possible pour faire tout ce que vous m'avez dit de faire, seigneur.

In the first phrase of the first excerpt, we have a nice pattern of high front rounded, high front unrounded, and high back rounded vowels punctuated by voiceless dental stops forming a parallel structure.

> Plus vite que tout de suite
>   y it   tu t   yit

The "forty eight kicks", referred to in the first quote, is a hyperbolic description of the beating this man will suffer and the place of the beating is, of course, the posterior which is named by a figurative term in Walloon, "panê-cou." The excerpt ends with an alliteration of /k/ sounds.

> caisse aux cliquottes
> k   k k

The second excerpt shows a very different use of language. The old knight is addressed with "tu" but he responds using formal style repeating "faire" (and its variant "faisant") five times in this very short speech. He also uses "seigneur" three times and "vous" twice, referencing the addressee far more often than he does himself, even though he is answering a question concerning his own actions. Unlike the first excerpt, the linguistic form of this speech is remarkable in its uncreative repetitiveness and lack of information. That, in itself, is not funny, but when taken in context, we laugh at the old knight who is so obedient to and respectful of authority that he has lost the ability to think for himself. This character provides a fine contrast to the irascible Tchantchès who generally addresses Charlemagne with "tu" and is always ready to stand up for his rights.

Tchantchès characters frequently deform words and proper names, pretending that they have simply misunderstood.[9] For example, someone calls Tchantchès "Impertinent" and he replies "My name's not Ferdinand, it's Tchantchès." The parallelism between these two words is great. The two consonants that differ do so in voicing only. Simple nouns that are deformed may be valid words in their final form (e.g. garçon maçon, hommages fromages) or they may turn into nonsense words (e.g. château chaspiteau, cercueil certicueil, princesse prinçoisse). Proper names may undergo more alterations, but they are always turned into words or phrases with specific referents (e.g. Isabelle Escabelle, Oger Horloger, Lucifer L'homme qui flaire).

Another trick which is used by Pinet (and also English punchmen) is having Tchantchès declare that he cannot say a certain word which he proceeds to pronounce in the same sentence.

TCHANTCHES: S'il vous plat. S'il vous plaît—je ne sais jamais dire s'il vous plait hein moi.
KNIGHT: Mais tu viens de le dire ami.

The word which Tchantchès claims not to be able to pronounce might be the correct version of a word he just mispronounced (e.g. "s'il vous plat" for "s'il vous plaît" in the above example) or it might be a word that is considered impolite (e.g. crevé instead of fatigué). In the first case, he feels that he is prevented from saying the word correctly due to his physical abilities and in the second case because of the norms of politeness. Tchantchès always acts surprised when the character sharing the stage with him informs him that he just said the word in question.

Pinet's plays are rich in word play with bodily referents. Most instances of word play in his shows take the form of set phrases which have been handed down through generations of Pinets, although they appear in puppet shows outside the Pinet family as well. One example is "je me suis trompeté" for "je me suis trompé." The former sentence, by merely adding one extra syllable onto the standard way of saying "I am wrong", translates as "I am trumpeted." While this does not make sense in any narrow meaning of the words, the connotational meanings point clearly to flatulence. Support for the association between musical instruments and flatulence comes in a play by Dufour where Tchantchès reminds Nanesse that she has eaten gas-producing food and he does not want to hear her clarinets playing all night. This debasement of elements of high culture, musical instruments used in symphonies and, in the case of the trumpet, to announce official proclamations, is a trademark of folk humor as brought out in Bakhtin's perspicacious treatment of Rabelais.[10] Another illustration of this is Pinet's Tchantchès announcing "J'ai fait mes latrines et mes humidités à l'Université de St. Pholien." Only three phonemes are altered in the first part of the phrase, yet the sense of the words is radically changed.

mes latrines et mes humidités
ɸ   an

From two quite elevated subjects in the university curriculum, Latin and Humanities, are derived "toilets" and "dampness." Once again the high culture is debased and reference is made to the anal section of the body. The phrase ends with a sort of oxymoron which also debases an institution of high culture, for not only is there no university in the Liège quarter of St. Pholien, but it is a distinctly working class quarter whose inhabitants have little to do with the city's university. Pinet's Tchantchès also makes numerous references to other bodily functions, whether being pissed on by the baby Jesus or reminding the audience at intermission that the toilet paper is free.

Deville also includes a large dose of folk or carnivalesque humor in his plays, which is appropriate since he generally performs at carnivals. In one of his plays, Tchantchès is confronted by the green monster of the swamp. He promptly defecates and when his knightly companion asks if he was scared, he replies, "Oh oui hein, mon seigneur, que j'ai eu peur et je sens hein mon seigneur, que j'ai fait d' la moutarde dans mon panê-cou moi mon seigneur et que ça coule comme des petits pois hors d'une boîte de Marie Thumas." ("Oh yes sir, I was scared and I feel, sir, that I've made mustard in my shirt tails, sir, and that it's oozing out like peas out of a can of Marie Thumas," a famous Belgian canning company). With this incident, we are reminded of Rabelais (Book 4, Chapter 67) as quoted by Bakhtin: "One of the symptoms and mishaps of fear is that it usually opens the back door of the rotunda where fecal guests await their turn to emerge."[11] There is a play on the Walloon word "panê-cou" which means "shirt tail" literally and "coward" figuratively, linking the location and cause of defecation in a single word. We also cannot overlook the fact that the two substances he compares his feces with are both foodstuffs, mustard and peas. An even more direct link between feces and food is made by Pinet's father in a recording of a play he performed in 1950. In this play, a tchantchès showing someone his youngest child remarks how he is first playing with his feces and then sticking it in his mouth.

A fixation on the oral, especially with respect to food, accompanies the anal fixation. Whenever two Tchantchès talk to each other in Pinet's shows, the conversation frequently revolves around food and drink, usually referencing one of the local specialties like French fries, "bouquettes",[12] and especially "pèkèt." A couple of the standard word plays have food referents. For instance, "et moi aussi" "et moi saucisse" and "Je présente mes hommages" "Je présente mes fromages." Furthermore, the name of Pinet's most popular Tchantchès is Biscuit—a food name in the tradition of Hanswurst, John Pickle Herring, Jean Potage, etc.

Besides defecation, food, and drink, the last basic area of bodily folk humor addressed by Bakhtin is sex and procreation. For the most part, it appears to be the least represented topic of interest in the Liège puppet theater. The sexual matters that arise in the plots of the stories performed by the puppeteers are excised from the puppet performances. The puppeteers seem to agree that they are playing predominantly for children and that the sexual exploits of puppet characters are not suitable material. However, indirect and humorous allusions to sex and procreation survive among the tchantchès. Procreation in its hyperbolic form is evident in the portrayal of the "Massacre of the Innocents" when Herod's soldiers ask different tchantchès how many children they have. The tchantchès answer with numbers like forty and one hundred thirty seven. Here, we are reminded of Polichinelle's companion, Dame Gigogne, who constantly gave birth to children on stage.

Other allusions to sex have less direct links with procreation. In one of the chivalric plays, Pinet's Tchantchès tells Duke Aymon that he will not go hunting with him because boars have horns and if they stick you in the backside they tear your pants. He does not like drafts in his pants because they cool off his ardor and his wife screams at him at night. In Deville's theater, Tchantchès asks Lucifer if he knows why devils have horns. Lucifer says he doesn't know and Tchantchès looks at the audience and says sarcastically "They must have happy home lives with such horns." He then proceeds to beat him up, figuratively cuckolding the devil.

The tchantchès are privileged as the only characters who make sexual allusions, thus linking them with procreation. They are also linked with its opposite, death. Some puppeteers say that Tchantchès does not kill others in battle, he only knocks them out or puts them to sleep. It is quite possible that this is a reaction to modern day parents who complain about excessive violence in the puppet theater. Whether Tchantchès kills or not, it is still the lower class comic characters who are generally responsible for burying the dead.[13] The standard phrase they speak to the audience when they appear on stage to accomplish this task is: "Now I must care for the dead and bury the wounded." The audience objects and corrects him. Often they yell "It's the reverse!" in which case Tchantchès answers, "Oh, I must bury the wounded and care for the dead." They continue to object until he gets it right. In some theaters, Tchantchès mentions making some kind of food out of the bodies, bringing the imagery back around to the oral, and life-giving substances.

Oaths are a favorite comic device which come to the forefront in Deville's theater with variations on "Oh Sainte Bablène tote plaquée de crotales de gade!" (Oh Saint Bablène all plastered with goat turds). The imagery links the supernatural with the animal and the anal. These oaths are directed at the general state of affairs, not at a particular individual. Sometimes however, characters are singled out to be made fun of. The leading Tchantchès is the only one who pokes fun in this manner and it is generally directed at other tchantchès or at evil characters who are not completely human. The case mentioned above concerning the devil having horns is an example of this as are the times Tchantchès tauntingly asks an unclothed skeleton with completely exposed teeth which tailor or dentist he frequents.

In the Nativity play where several tchantchès play the roles of shepherds and a shepherdess filing in to see the baby Jesus, the leading tchantchès insults each of his friends as they approach the baby. In Dufour's play, after the leading tchantchès pays his respects, Djètrou is the first to approach the child with the following words, "Ah ké bè nozé gningnin. Il a tot-a-fêt les oûys di s' papa. Peut-on bien le bähî, Madame?" (Oh what a pretty little crybaby. He has exactly the same eyes as his father. Could I kiss him, Madame?) Mary agrees, but Tchantchès steps in telling Djètrou not to forget that she has eaten onions and she could make the baby sick with her bad breath. He tells the next shepherd to be careful that the fleas from his beard do not fall on the baby. When the following visitor remarks that the baby Jesus has mistaken him for his father, Tchantchès responds incredulously, "with your false teeth that lift up when you laugh? Careful that they don't fall in the baby's mouth." Tchantchès yells at the fourth visitor to remove the wad of tobacco from his mouth because he is slobbering on the baby and he instructs the last one, who has a prominent nose, not to go near the baby for fear the baby will mistake his nose for a bottle.

In all these cases, the allusions are to the body. Three of these refer to the mouth, that privileged cavity in folk humor which consumes over and above what is needed to keep a body alive. The introduction of substances into the mouth serves as the first stage in the eventual defecation process. However, these three allusions are to substances coming out of the mouth (bad breath, teeth, and saliva) representing, in a way, the reverse of defecation, or the expulsion of things from the opposite end of the body. All these allusions also indicate a certain lack of personal care and hygiene as is also the case with the fleas in the other shepherd's beard. Lastly, the enormous nose is an obvious manifestation of the exaggeration of physical features. This is a common practice in folk humor and in the puppet theater in particular where the entire actor is created out of inanimate materials, so the creator is free to carve his characters as disproportionately and as grotesquely as he likes. Furthermore, the puppeteers see a connection between the way a puppet looks and the way it talks. Often the most grotesque looking puppets are the ones with the strangest voices.

In many of the comic instances that have been mentioned thus far, incongruity comes to the foreground. This appears to be a basic trait of comedy in general, though various cultures may differ on what they perceive as incongruous. Incongruity creates strange images in the listener's mind, like false teeth falling into a baby's mouth, and these images make us laugh. Take, for instance the following example from Pinet's Tchantchès after he has been given permission to lead the King's army: "Allez! Bataillons! Attention! Enlevez vos pantalons![14] Non non non non non non non!" It is incongruous first of all that Tchantchès would be leading a royal army. Secondly, the statement is incongruous in and of itself since it begins in a very serious manner and then commands the troops to do something utterly ridiculous. Of all the things Tchantchès could have commanded the troops to do, few would have been as absurd as asking them to take their pants off. Again, this shows a fixation on the nether parts. Lastly, after Tchantchès gives the command, he immediately retracts it, another incongruous action. It is left to our imaginations whether he retracts it so quickly because he is afraid of receiving the wrath of the king, or whether the troops are actually removing their pants, or both. In any case, the statement is funny due to its incongruity on several accounts.

Playing with frames

Anachronism is an incongruity of time frames created by mixing elements from vastly different time periods into a single time period. It is a technique which is used liberally by most puppeteers since the sudden shift of time frames that it effects is regarded as humorous. For instance, a peasant in the nativity play declares that his wheat has grown as high as a telephone pole, or Tchantchès exclaims that they must call up the fire department when Hernier de la Seine sets fire to the castle of the Four Sons of Aymon. Many of these anachronisms are formulaic expressions like many of the humorous interjections mentioned earlier. Others are created immediately before, or even during, performance and may refer to events read about in that day's newspaper. Political satire, while sometimes inserted into Tchantchès' speech before the story begins, is just as likely to be slipped into the story in the form of anachronism. An example of this takes place during a scene in which Charlemagne, seeing that the war is over, announces that he will distribute food to all the peasants in the countryside. Tchantchès asks him in Walloon, "How are you going to pay for it with the devaluation?" The devaluation of the Belgian franc was the hottest topic of conversation at that point in time, so the joke was well received. This, however, could not become a set comic phrase like the two examples mentioned earlier which have much wider temporal references.

Since puppet shows occur inside a well-defined frame, there is a humorous effect to any breaking of that frame, as we have seen in the discussion of anachronism. Other types of frame breaks involve puppets trying to join the realm of humans by discussing personal traits of members of the audience, and people who temporarily lose sight of the nature of the puppets. In the first case, puppets insinuate that they have contact with the audience members outside the frame of the theater thus suggesting that, although puppets, they lead normal human lives. In the second case, people in the audience get caught up in the action of the puppet shows until they think themselves actors in the show. Both these aspects of the puppet show will be looked at in the following paragraphs.

Dufour's Tchantchès is his only character who speaks directly to the audience. In this capacity, both a pedantic streak and a trickster quality emerge. The moralist side of Tchantchès usually emerges through the reported speech of parents who come backstage before the show and tell Dufour any particular problems they are having with a certain child. Dufour cleverly works into Tchantchès' introductory speech a public reprimand to this child for being lazy, not eating well, lying, or the like. Tchantchès first tells the story which brings to light the undesirable trait and does not mention the person's name until the end. If the description is well constructed, some laughter will follow when he finishes (nervous laughter if several people think the description fits them). Then, when he names the person, the audience laughs much harder. This technique works best if the audience and puppeteer are familiar with each other which is usually the case in neighborhood puppet theaters but is not normally the case at the museum where Dufour performs. At one show I attended, however, Dufour did know several people in the audience and they all knew each other, being members of a class of future teachers of Walloon. In his introductory speech, Tchantchès first made fun of one man's regional accent, then chided a certain woman for being shy and then he went into a story about a friend of his who told him they would go out for a drink next time he saw him because, like all good Liégeois, he likes to buy old friends drinks when he sees them. "This friend is here in the room" said Tchantchès "but he never came to say hello." He paused and then loudly exclaimed that it was because he didn't want to buy the drinks. There was slight laughter in the audience but it increased fourfold after Tchantchès called out, "Isn't that right, M. Leduc?" M. Leduc publically admitted to being a cheapskate.

It is in repartees such as this that the puppeteer and the puppet become inseparable and the puppet seems to be insisting that he really is human by possessing knowledge that only a human involved in normal social relations could possess. The incongruity of this has a humorous effect. A further incongruity of these playful repartees is that while this character possesses human knowledge, he is not bound by the same rules of social interaction since he is, after all, only a puppet. Therefore he is allowed to air someone's personal qualities in public without fear of angry retribution. This interaction in which Tchantchès tries to establish himself as a member of the human community takes place before the play begins and therefore stands outside the story frame, though it forms an integral part of the puppet show as a whole. Within the story frame of the puppet show, the human/puppet division is also periodically effaced through the engrossment of the audience members.

In Libert's theater, there is a high level of participation between the puppets and the audience throughout the show. The children are completely absorbed in his plays, whether yelling for Tchantchès, advising characters on what to do or answering questions from the puppet characters. The puppeteer listens closely to what they have to say and even makes them believe that they are the ones directing the action of the play. Occasionally one child will become so engrossed that he or she will urgently yell something above the noise of the crowd directed specifically to the puppets as if no one else were in the room. The adults find this "flooding out" of the children extremely amusing. [15] In fact, due to audience arrangement, with children occupying the first few rows and adults in the back, the frame of the "show" watched by the adults is much larger than that which encloses the puppets. The adults watch the puppets and the children together. The reaction of the children to the puppets is often as amusing as the antics of the puppets themselves.

While adults, too, may get so engrossed that they misframe the puppet show, they are more likely to keep their misrecognition to themselves as a source of private amusement. Exceptions to this are well known in the puppet world. Take for instance the numerous stories which involve a member of the audience attacking the puppet villain.[16] Of course, the most famous incident of this sort is Don Quixote who draws his sword and rescues Don Gaiferos from the Moorish puppets.

The types of frame-breaking which have been discussed so far occur within temporal frames or within the constituted area of puppet/audience interaction. The audience wants to know that they are watching puppets which are acting like humans. In other words, their actions and reactions, though highly stylized, are reminiscent of human actions and reactions. The audience members are amused when they discover that they have been perceiving the puppets as humans, not as puppets acting like humans. In a successful show, the audience members oscillate back and forth between these two perceptions. Once in a while, however, the puppets stop acting like humans and instead act exactly like puppets.

For instance, a knight marching regally across stage suddenly drops his leg and continues marching as if nothing had happened. The shock causes great hilarity in the audience, but unlike the humor mentioned so far, this is unintended by the puppeteer. Also unintended by the puppeteer is the humorous effect created when the audience can hear him yelling at his assistants backstage during a show. These two events are seen as humorous by most people though, admittedly, some find them merely distracting.

Other types of unintended humor occur when there is a disjunction between the puppeteer and the audience. In Liège, as elsewhere in Europe, the disjunction usually occurs along class lines, as the upper class becomes interested in regional folklore. In this case, the upper class observer finds great hilarity in the fact that Charlemagne and other nobles speak with lower class accents. The puppeteer, however, is speaking in the most correct French he can muster. The observer is mocking the art form and, indeed, the puppeteer himself and there is no way that the puppeteer can turn it around so that he is in control of the humor.

With other "accidents" that occur on stage, the puppeteer, if he notices on time, can turn them into even funnier scenes under his control. This is what happened when Pinet's Tchantchès lost his entire body on stage in Munich, Germany. Pinet was left with Tchantchès' head floating at the end of the steel rod. He immediately had Tchantchès turn to the audience and say "Gee, it seems I've lost my body. Oh well, it's better than losing your head." "To lose your body" has only a literal meaning and it is hard to imagine a scenario in which it might be used. "To lose your head," on the contrary, has a clear reference to "going crazy." In fact, in English, French, German, and several other languages, this non-literal meaning is far more common than the literal one. Tchantchès was assuring the audience that although he had physically fallen apart, he was still mentally together. The repartee continued as Tchantchès asked about the quality of hospitals in Munich. The audience howled with laughter, but it was not at the expense of the puppeteer.

Genre

So far, we have looked at aspects of the puppet theater that have an instant comical effect. But what about the genre of the puppet play as a whole? On this level, we cannot isolate a single peal of laughter that might prove the play a comedy or a parody. We must use a wider lens. First, it might be asked whether the plays based on classical literature, most notably the *chansons de geste*, are not all parodies. After all, as Lindsay has noted, marionettes are instruments of parody par excellence.[17] Some of the classical puppet plays are performed tongue in cheek, but after the sincere belief in and reverence toward the medieval plots and characters shown me by some liégeois puppeteers, I can hardly consider all chivalric puppet shows as parodies of the genre. Instead, they are often considered true portrayals of history. Nevertheless, many puppeteers have the tchantchès perform comic dialogue within these shows even while maintaining a respectful attitude toward the historic material. It also seems to be quite common to include a short comic skit in the program beside a more serious historical play. We can find allusions to these short comic skits in old accounts of the puppet shows, but they were always considered unimportant by the researchers and were not described, as were the religious plays and the plays of the *chansons de geste*.

Gaston Engels, who grew up with a puppet theater in his living room, says that his father used to perform shorter comedies between the longer, more serious episodes based on nineteenth century renditions of medieval literature. When he began performing at the fairs in 1927, he took up the comic genre because the serial nature of the medieval stories did not fit his new, rapidly changing audience. True to comic form, these short plays always end with a prelude to an upcoming marriage.[18] This genre is continued in the work of Deville.

Libert, who performed puppet shows while a prisoner of war in Germany in which Mussolini and Hitler suffered the wrath of Tchantchès, is one puppeteer known for his comedies and his parodies of classical literary works. He once did a parody of Romeo and Juliette in which Romeo was a boy from Outre Meuse and Juliette was an Italian immigrant's daughter. He also performed an adult comedy in Walloon called "Voyage to the Orient." In this play, Tchantchès wins a lottery which gives him a trip to the Middle East.[19] He packs a few things including a large stewpot ("casserole") which he ties on his back. When he disembarks in the Middle East, he is hungry and starts muttering something about getting out his "casserole" and making a meal. Meanwhile, a group of disgruntled Arabs are waiting at the airport for a Latin American revolutionary who will help them overthrow the government. They hear Tchantchès muttering about his "casserole" and say to each other "That must be him, Fidel Casserole." The story develops around the mistaken identity of Tchantchès and is comic from start to finish.

Conclusion

From the comic plays performed by Libert and Deville to the comic interjections in serious plays exemplified in the work of Dufour and Pinet, humor is an important resource for Liégeois puppeteers. The very basis for this humor lies in incongruity: in the imagery of bodily functions as instruments of degradation, in gross exaggeration, and in incidences of frame-breaking. We have seen the various forms humor can take in the Liège puppet shows, from voice quality to word play and beyond. Now we will look at the various functions it fulfills.

First of all, people like to laugh, so a show that is known to be funny will be well attended. Consequently, humor is important to the puppeteer for it functions as an entertaining device to draw an audience. During the show, it has an additional function as an indicator of audience involvement. It is important for entertainers to know that the audience is engaged in the performance. Actors on a stage can see this in the faces and actions of their audience. Puppeteers and their audiences are hidden from each other and therefore it is doubly important for the puppeteer to receive vocal cues as to how his audience is reacting to the show.

In a less mechanical vein, comedy allows us to question the conventions by which we live., These conventions, which we might call "culture" in its anthropological sense and, more specifically, "Culture" in the sense of upper class mores, are thought so necessary as to be a part of nature. Comic characters show the world that cultural norms are not fixed in nature, but they can be played around with, and they can even be subverted by biological functions. Their special relationship with the audience draws the spectators into this comical way of looking at the world, a world in which an unarmed commoner wipes out whole armies of armored knights, a world in which eating and drinking are more important than attending school, a world which confounds the natural and supernatural, feces and food, life and death.

And who are these comic characters but members of the peasant or working class, the people who suffer most from the way the conventions presently work. Comedy is their particular way of speaking which is base, clever, and most of all, irreverent. For in these comic exchanges, class divisions are negated. Commoners address the king with "tu" and order royal armies to remove their pants. As garments, and in particular, uniforms, are stripped away, so are the culturally imposed inequalities that exist in society and we are reduced to unadorned biological specimens.

I will not hazard a guess as to whether the type of humor which forms the basis of this paper contributes to the maintenance of cultural norms by working as a sort of "steam valve" which releases built up tension, or whether its function is, instead, counter hegemonic. Certainly, it could work in either way, but this is a much more complex question which involves a far larger context than that which is addressed in this paper. Suffice it to say that the puppet theater, though only a small part of society as a whole, is deeply rooted in society and has a symbolic value that far outreaches the domain of the theater.

Notes

[1]A discussion of framebreaking can be found in Erving Goffman, *Frame Analysis* (Cambridge: Harvard University Press, 1974).

[2]It is essential that any investigation of humor in the Liège puppet theater be based on live performances since humorous parts are seldom written in the scripts, but are improvised in performance, often in conjunction with audience repartee.

[3]Dell Hymes, "Ways of Speaking," in *Explorations in the Ethnography of Speaking*, ed. by Richard Bauman and Joel Sherzer (New York: Cambridge University Press, 1974), pp. 433-451.

[4]Since Tchantchès stands in for the puppeteer on stage, he can be seen as the "human cohort" in puppet form and in this role he manipulates how one is to interpret the story. Gerold Hanck, "A Frame Analysis of the Puppet Theater" (unpublished paper, University of Pennsylvania) p. 8.

[5]All of the puppeteers claimed that they used their natural voice for Tchantchès. Although this is never actually the case, Tchantchès' voice is devoid of the various speech defects and non-liégeois accents that mark the other tchantchès.

[6]J.K. Chambers and Peter Trudgill, *Dialectology* (New York: Cambridge University Press, 1980) pp. 186-189.

[7]For examples of comic puppet characters speaking in regional, non-standard dialect while the other characters speak a more standard variety in Malaysia, see Amin Sweeney, *The Ramayana and the Malay Shadow-Play* (Kuala Lumpur: National University of Malaysia Press, 1972), p. 63; in Sicily, see Antonio Pasqualino, *L'Opera dei Pupi* (Palermo: Sellerio Editore, 1977), p. 87, and "Marionettes and glove puppets: Two theatrical systems of Southern Italy," *Semiotica*, 47(1/4, 1983), pp. 235-236; in Torino, Italy, see Roberto Leydi, "Les marionnettes en Italie," in *Les Marionnettes*, ed. by Paul Fournel (Paris: Bordas, 1982), p. 20; in Lyon, France, see Paul Fournel, "Le Guignol lyonnais" in *Les Marionnettes*, ed. by Paul Fournel (Paris: Bordas, 1982), p. 38; in Amiens, France, see Reginald Sibbald, *Marionettes in the North of France* (Philadelphia: University of Pennsylvania Press, 1936), p. 59; in Roubaix, France, see Léopold Delannoy, *Théâtres de Marionnettes du Nord de la France* (Paris: Maisonneuve et Larose, 1983), p. 135; in Lille, France, see ibid, p. 64; and in Brussels, Belgium, see Antoinette Botsford, *The Toone Marionette Theater of Brussels* (Ann Arbor: University Microfilms, 1983), p. 110.

[8]Edward Remouchamps, *Tåtî l' Pèriquî* (Liège: Vaillant-Carmanne, 1885).

[9]See Frank Proschan, "Puppet voices and interlocutors: Language in folk puppetry," *Journal of American Folklore*, 94(1981), pp. 527-555, for examples of this sort of word play in the English Punch and Russian Petroushka traditions.

[10]Mikhail Bakhtin, *Rabelais and his World* (Cambridge: M.I.T. Press, 1968).

[11]ibid, p. 174.

[12]A "bouquette" is a thick crepe made during the Christmas season.

[13]In the Javanese Wayang it is also the vulgar clowns who deal with the dead bodies, James Brandon, *On Thrones of Gold: Three Javanese Shadow Plays* (Cambridge: Harvard University Press, 1970), p. 323, and let us not forget Shakespeare's grave-digging clowns in *Hamlet*.

[14]It is quite possible that this is a parodic combination of the chorus of the French national anthem "Aux armes, citoyens. Formez vos bataillons...." and the popular movement "les sans culottes" which came into existence after the French Revolution. I thank André Lefevere for this insight.

[15]Goffman. pp. 350-359.

[16]For an example of this type of frame breaking, see Paul McPharlin, *Puppet Theater in America, 1524 to Now* (New York: Harper's, 1949), p. 204.

[17]Frank W. Lindsay, *Dramatic Parody in 18th century Paris* (New York: King's Crown Press, 1946).

[18]Maurice Charney, *Comedy High and Low: An Introduction to the Experience of Comedy* (New York: Oxford University Press, 1978).

[19]The theme of the winning lottery ticket, we recall, is also central in the older Walloon comedy, *Tätî l' Pèriqû*. The lottery was mentioned in Foster's discussion of the theory of limited good as one of the few ways Mexican villagers explained the inequality of wealth in a community, George Foster, *Tzintzuntzan: Mexican peasants in a changing world* (Boston: Little Brown, 1967). The Liégeois working class is well aware of the means by which wealth is produced and therefore does not see it as limited; however, they do know that their access to it is highly restricted.

Humor and Anti-Humor in Western Puebloan Puppetry Performances

M. Jane Young

Western Puebloan[1] puppetry performances occur within the context of an annual cycle of sacred dramas that serve as symbolic enactments of world view and include personifications of powerful beings who control all aspects of existence.[2] The performers are generally men who have been initiated into the sacred Kachina Society; the performing objects integral to these dramatic enactments include masks, ritual paraphernalia and puppets (described in most of the ethnographic literature as "effigies"); the audience consists of those tribal members who are not directly involved in the performance. Members of the religious societies encourage community attendance at such performances and, in fact, regard it as a responsibility because it is important to have many minds concentrating or meditating on the sacred nature of the event.[3] The "presentness" of the past is implicit in such performances; as the ritual drama takes place, the puppets and other performing objects, especially the kachina masks, become powerful, affecting presences that evoke the time of the myth. These objects are, therefore, metonymic of events of the myth time; in the context of the performance, the part stands for and evokes the presence of the whole, and the past becomes one with the present.[4]

Ritual drama functions to reinforce Western Puebloan world view; it operates both as a vehicle for the enactment of behavior that supports that world view and behavior that challenges that particular vision of reality. An example of the former, the presentation of behavior that ought to occur, is the dramatic representation of the sun's motion through the sky—a part of the winter solstice ceremony at the Hopi village of Oraibi. In this performance, "the 'Star priest' twirls the sun symbol very fast...symbolizing the going and coming of the sun."[5] Thus behavior appropriate to the sun is dramatically depicted; it travels across the sky daily from east to west; furthermore, it turns around at the winter solstice and moves northward along the horizon towards the summer solstice position, warming the fields and air so that the crops will grow. On the other hand, one group of the Zuni "clowns," the Mudheads (*Koyemshi*), frequently exemplify behavior in ritual drama that should not happen in daily life. During the summer rain dances, they mimic the kachinas (deified ancestors impersonated by members of the religious societies) and make obscene gestures to the highly respected matrons of the tribe.[6] This behavior is humorous precisely because it is a ritual reversal or inversion of appropriate behavior; the audience members laugh, but there is an element of "shock" in that laughter. Such a performance embodies not only humor, but anti-humor; it permits a vision of the chaos that is ever ready to impinge on daily life should the necessary rituals and the attendant proper behavior be neglected; it is a vehicle through which the comic and the mysterious are intertwined. Similarly, the two types of behavior enacted are not entirely separate; frequently they occur as integral elements of the same performance, and the boundaries between the two are not always clearly defined. The same principle extends to the puppetry performances: although much of the behavior that is characteristic of these performances is quite serious and, in fact, even dangerous, humor is also implicit in these performances, but it is generally the dangerous aspect of humor that is exemplified.

Although my focus is on puppetry in ritual drama, I will briefly describe the role of the Mudheads, a group of Western Puebloan "clowns," as well, because they play a significant role in one of the major puppetry performances of the Hopi and are frequently associated with the Horned Water Serpent at both Hopi and Zuni.

Mudheads (Koyemshi)

According to Zuni mythology, the Mudheads are the result of the incestuous union of a brother and sister during the search to find "the center."[7] The parents who commit this transgression and their offspring become hideous, non-human beings who lose the ability to speak properly. They go about almost naked and their heads are covered with unsightly knobs of mud. The grotesque nature of the act is mirrored in the grotesque appearance of these beings, the result of behavior which is antithetical to culture and society. Similarly, the Mudheads often take on a role in ritual drama that is oppositional to tribal norms.[8] They are buffoon-like in appearance and action, mocking accepted behavior, even mimicking the sacred, stately kachinas. The audience laughs openly at their antics and this laughter seems to drive the Mudheads to new excesses; but the Mudheads play a serious and powerful role as well. Zunis talk of them with respect and fear, saying "one must never refuse anything to the *Koyemshi* because they are dangerous"; they frequently attribute accidents they experience to improprieties toward these "clowns."[9] The knobs on the heads and packets under the neckcloths of the *Koyemshi* contain the seeds of plants that are vital to Western Puebloan agricultural practice and ceremonialism, representing their association with fertility. Furthermore, Zunis say these knobs also contain dust that the Mudheads collect from the footprints of townspeople;[10] some of the power that the Mudheads have over people is derived from the metonymic quality of the footprint, for it embodies the essence of the individual. The Mudheads augment this power by putting black butterfly wings, which, according to Zuni belief, drive people mad with sexual obsession, in the drums that they carry.[11]

Although the Mudheads perform hilarious clown routines during the summer rain dances when the kachina dancers have left the plaza to rest, they become quite sober when the kachinas return. As the kachinas dance and sing, the Mudheads act as directors of the performance, shouting out critical comments that are heeded by the performers; they also take on the role of interpreters, miming the words of the songs for the audience.[12] In addition, the "father" of the Mudheads stands next to the dance leader of the kachinas during the "serious" part of the rain dances and listens to him recite the sacred prayers.[13] The Mudheads also watch over the kachina impersonators as they dance and adjust parts of their costumes that come undone. Finally, the Zuni clowns may ritually enact, in a "humorous" context, serious objections to the behavior of others, in a manner that serves as a critique of that behavior. For example, in the early 1970s they performed the drama of the first moon walk as a protest to this "rape" of the Moon Mother.[14] Thus, the behavior and appearance of the Mudheads embody both humor and anti-humor, components of their participation in puppetry performances as well.

Western Puebloan puppets[15]

To a certain extent, the characterization of "puppet" depends upon the limits one puts on the definition. For instance, the more encompassing term, "performing objects," would certainly refer to masks as well, but the focus herein is on entire figures, representing personages or animals, which an actor manipulates.[16] According to this definition, the puppets most frequently employed by the Western Puebloans are representations of the Horned Water Serpent, a mythological being who plays a major role in their ceremonialism and religion.[17] Not only is he/she the guardian of sacred springs, but the Horned Water Serpent has rain-bringing power that can operate in excess to bring floods as well. Conceived of as both individual and multiple, the Horned Water Serpent is frequently depicted in Zuni visual art in association with the six directions: the points of winter and summer solstice sunrise and sunset as well as the zenith and nadir.[18] It is noteworthy that the puppetry performance at the Hopi village of Walpi described below includes six serpents in some of the acts. The puppet performances that center around the Horned Water Serpent also sometimes feature certain bird puppets as well as maiden "marionettes" who grind corn.[19]

The Hopi call the Horned Water Serpent *Palulukong*; the Zuni counterpart is *Kolowisi*. Both groups most frequently represent the Horned Water Serpent in ritual drama as an effigy or puppet, a mechanical contrivance somewhat like a small Chinese dragon with bulging eyes, a central horn curving forward at the top of the head and a ruff of feathers about the neck (Figure 1).[20] This is an unusual mode of depiction—most other Hopi and Zuni gods impersonated in ritual drama are represented by masks.[21]

Horned Water Serpent puppets play a major role in the *Palulukonti*, a Hopi ritual drama centering on fertility which is held in late February or early March, timed to occur before the spring planting of crops.[22] As the actors enter the kiva (a ceremonial chamber, sometimes circular and generally subterranean) with a rolled up cloth screen and other paraphernalia, the fire tender holds a blanket in front of the flames so that the kiva is in shadows while the stage is set. A major component of several acts of the performance is the elaborately decorated screen, suspended by ropes from the roof of the kiva, through which hidden puppeteers thrust the puppets. Sometimes the screen contains six circular disks: the largest and most central disk represents the sun while two smaller disks on either side of this sun, distinguished by crescents, represent the moon; the other three disks are sun symbols. The disks are hinged at the top and they move upward as the serpent puppets plunge forward; ethnologist J.W. Fewkes regards this action as representing the antagonistic relationship which exists between the sun and the Horned Water Serpent in Western Puebloan thought.[23] The screen contains a number of other painted images, including depictions of humans, birds, rain clouds, lightning, and falling rain. Prior to the enactment of the drama, members of certain kachina societies grow corn plants in heated kivas; then they attach them to clay pedestals which they place in front of the screen, creating a miniature field of corn. In certain of the acts a wooden framework is used instead of the screen; a hidden puppeteer manipulates bird puppets so that they walk back and forth across the top of this framework to the accompaniment of bird calls performed by one of the actors. The effigy manipulators or puppeteers remain hidden from the audience, behind the screen or wooden framework, throughout the entire performance.

Figure 1. Kolowisi (Zuni plumed serpent) with head thrust through tablet that is used in initiation ceremony. Photograph taken by Matilda C. Stevenson in the 1890s. (Courtesy Smithsonian Institution, National Anthropological Archives).

The serpent puppets are generally four or five feet long, manipulated by means of a rod called the "back bone." The men who make the puppets attach to them, on the backbone, a few inches back from the neck, a quartz crystal called the "heart," a package containing seeds of important crops as well as corn kernels in the colors of the six directions, and a black prayer stick. They make the heads of the serpents out of gourds, to which they add the central, forward-curving horn, goggle eyes, and ruff of feathers described above; they carve jagged teeth for the serpents' mouths, adding red-painted, protruding leather tongues. It is of note that, just as they do with the "heart," the makers of the puppets put "typical" seeds of corn and other important plants in the goggle eyes of the serpents (at both Hopi and Zuni, ritual specialists also put such seeds in the goggle eyes of the kachina masks). They paint the heads and backs of the serpents black and color the bellies white, decorating them with semi-circular designs representing scales. Six of these puppets generally perform together. One, much larger than the others, takes the role of "mother"; it has eight mammae that the puppet makers stuff with corn kernels and seeds of cotton, melon, watermelon, and gourds (the same seeds they put in the "heart" and eyes). A hidden man who blows through a gourd creates the roar of the serpent in these performances; the Hopis say this sound is the "voice" of the water. Other hidden actors sing throughout the performance.[24]

Description of Performance

The performance of the *Palulukonti* drama entails a considerable amount of preparation on the part of the members of the sponsoring kachina society: they spend several days prior to the performance repainting and renovating the ritual paraphernalia, including the masks and serpent puppets; and they use the evenings for rehearsals in the kiva. Only those who are directly involved in the performance are admitted to the kiva at this time. The entire performance consists of several acts that combine to make one continuous performance lasting about three hours. Although all of the acts are undoubtedly of significance to an understanding of Western Puebloan ritual drama, I focus here only on those acts in which the actors employ puppets.[25]

Members of the chorus stand to either side of the screen and chant the notes of the song that signals the beginning of the first act. As the song continues, men wearing the masks and costumes of the Bear Kachinas dance. Then a concealed actor blows through an empty gourd, producing a hoarse roar that resounds from behind the screen; as the circular disks swing upwards, the six serpent puppets plunge simultaneously through the openings. Hopis describe these six as the mother, her two babies and three male serpents. As the song grows louder, the serpents move farther forward and swing back and forth in unison, raising and lowering their heads in time to the tempo of the song. They bite ferociously at each other and dart viciously at actors standing near the screen. Suddenly they bend their heads down to the floor and sweep across the imitation corn field, knocking over the clay pedestals and the corn plants that they contain. Then they raise their heads and again move them back and forth in unison. At this point, the "mother" serpent (the one with several udders on each side of her belly) suckles the others. J.W. Fewkes, who observed this performance at the Hopi village of Walpi in 1900, described the ensuing action as follows: "Meanwhile the roar emitted from behind the screen by a concealed man continued, and wild excitement seemed to prevail. Some of the spectators threw meal at the effigies, offering prayers, amid shouts from others."[26] Then the impersonator of the mother of all kachinas, *Hahai Wuhti*, who holds a basket of prayer meal, moves along in front of the projecting serpents, presenting each with prayer meal (for food) and then suckling each (Figure 2). Shortly after this, as the song diminishes in volume, the puppeteers draw the puppets back through the openings and the disks bearing the sun symbols fall down into place, as one final roar sounds from behind the screen. Members of the Kachina Society distribute the miniature corn plants to the women and girls among the spectators; the fire tenders again hold blankets in front of the flames to create concealing shadows as other participants remove the "set"; they roll the curtain up and the actors depart with their paraphernalia.

The serpent puppets appear again in the fifth and sixth acts, but, prior to that, in the third act, the audience is introduced to another type of puppet.[27] The focus of this act is on two marionettes representing the Corn Maidens; concealed actors skillfully manipulate these figures so that they appear to be grinding corn. The performers do not use a screen in this act; rather, they erect a wooden framework that surrounds the puppets like a stage in the center of the kiva. The girls move their bodies back and forth in time to the singing, as they grind corn meal on miniature *metates* (stone troughs). So realistic is this performance that the maidens even raise their hands to their faces and rub them with the meal, as do Hopi girls when grinding. As this marionette performance occurs, other puppeteers manipulate two bird puppets so that they walk back and forth along the upper horizontal bar of the stage, while bird calls emanate from the rear of the room. In a performance of this act observed by Fewkes in 1900, the kachina impersonators held "an animated conversation with the fire tenders, asserting that the girls were expert meal grinders, and from time to time crossed the room, putting pinches of the meal into the mouths of the fire tenders and spectators."[28] This act ends as did the previous one; amid the shadows, the participants

Figure 2. Hahai Wuhti offering corn meal to Horned Water Serpent puppets during a ritual at the Hopi Pueblo of Walpi. Drawing by M. Wright Gill, 1900. (Courtesy Smithsonian Institution, National Anthropological Archives).

Figure 3. Hopi Mudheads struggling with Horned Water Serpent puppets. Drawing by M. Wright Gill, 1900. (Courtesy Smithsonian Institution, National Anthropological Archives).

Figure 4. Horned Water Serpent puppets rising out of pottery jars behind miniature corn plants. Drawing by M. Wright Gill, 1900. (Courtesy Smithsonian Institution, National Anthropological Archives).

dismantle and carry out all of the paraphernalia. The marionettes appearing in this act operate as symbolic representations of the Corn Maidens who are central to Western Puebloan mythology; they bring gifts of corn and other seeds to the people. They are thus additional components of the network of symbolic associations focusing on fertility employed in this drama.

The fifth and sixth, or final, acts are similar to the first act in that the serpents knock over imitation fields of corn, but significantly differ in that Mudhead performers appear along with the serpents. In the fifth act, the screen is smaller, and decorated somewhat differently, but it still contains symbols that represent the sun. Only two serpents project from the sun disk openings. They are larger than those in the first performance, but are constructed in a similar manner. After the serpents knock over the corn plants, the Mudheads advance and wrestle with the snakes, but are frequently overcome and thrown to the floor (Figure 3). In one such performance, a Mudhead climbs on top of one of the serpents, "riding on its neck as if on horseback."[29] Finally, the serpents withdraw, accompanied by a prolonged roar, and the performance ends.

The performers do not use a screen in the sixth act. Instead, they place two pottery jars behind the miniature row of corn plants; a group of squatting Mudheads surrounds the jars and plants. The jars are decorated with symbols similar to those used on the screens: rain clouds, falling rain, four-pointed stars, and tadpoles.[30] As the chorus begins to sing, two artificial serpents rise slowly out of the jars (Figure 4). They are manipulated by hidden strings placed over the kiva rafters and again rise and fall, move backwards and forwards, in time to the music. As in the first and fifth acts when the actors employed screens, the serpents knock over the miniature fields of corn. Then they appear to struggle with each other, winding their heads together and performing other sorts of struggling motions. At the close of the performance, the effigies sink back into the jars and the song ends. As with the conclusions of previous acts, the fire tender holds a blanket over the flames as the actors depart with their paraphernalia, then other participants gather the small corn plants from the floor of the kiva and distribute them to the women and girls in the audience.

This performance does not always entail six acts. Indeed, six may constitute a somewhat abbreviated performance and the ethnographic literature includes accounts that describe as many as nine acts.[31] Of note is an additional act involving the six serpents and the screen: in this act one man stands in front of the screen and appears to struggle with a serpent puppet that he carries in his arms (sometimes several men enact this scenario). The actor manipulates the serpent puppet by concealing one arm in its body, while a false arm that he has tied to his shoulder in place of his hidden arm seems to grasp the serpent from the outside, deceiving the spectators. The performer then twists the puppet about his body and neck; sometimes he holds it above his head, or even throws it to the roof of the kiva, but all the while his appearance of desperately wrestling with the serpent is extremely realistic.[32]

Puppet Performances at the Pueblo of Zuni

At the Pueblo of Zuni, the Horned Water Serpent puppet performances are also of major significance, although they are not as elaborate as those at Hopi. The puppet itself is less complex mechanically; it is about five feet long, constructed of deerskin, and manipulated by a rod of cottonwood that extends through the puppet and symbolizes the spinal column.[33] The "heart" is represented by a miniature stick to which the creator of the puppet ties prayer feathers; he secures this stick to the middle of the long supporting rod. Further decoration of the serpent is quite similar to that of the Hopis, but at Zuni the performer who creates the serpent's roar blows through a conch shell rather than an empty gourd; the conch shell not only makes a harsh, resonant sound but also symbolizes the connection of the Horned Water Serpent with bodies of water.

At Zuni, *Kolowisi* appears primarily in a drama that occurs during the first initiation of boys who are between five and nine years old. Although it is not the vehicle for formal admittance of the boys as participants to the Kachina Society (that happens at another initiation that occurs when the boys are older), this ritual does serve to form a bond between the children and the kachinas.[34] Like the Horned Water Serpent performances at Hopi, this one at Zuni occurs in the early spring and centers symbolically on fertility, understood as a ritual request for long life for these young boys.[35] During parts of the initiation ritual, the Horned Water Serpent is accompanied by the female kachina, *Ahea*, the great-great-grandmother of the kachinas who, at one point, dances in the plaza and suckles *Kolowisi*. Although *Ahea* is said to bring long life, she is also associated with old age and death. Furthermore, like the Mudheads, she has a humorous side; sometimes when she dances she gets the songs mixed up and dances out of step.[36] The drama covers several days, beginning outside of town with the formation of a procession composed of the various performers who advance to the plaza, and concluding in one of the kivas with the Horned Water Serpent performance. During the procession into the village, *Kolowisi's* head projects from a large portable wooden tablet decorated with cloud symbols (Figure 1), rather than from an elaborate screen as at Hopi. The tablet is carried by two men who also carry spruce trees, symbolizing life and longevity. These spruce trees conceal the puppeteer and hide the conch shell trumpet that he blows to represent the roars of the serpent. Several of the kachinas accompany this procession, including the *Salimobia,* warrior gods and seed gatherers of the six directions who carry yucca whips with which they "urge" the initiates on to adulthood and long life. Later, in a performance in the plaza, the ceremonial father of each initiate carries the child on his back, passing in front of the kachinas who strike the child four times with bunches of yucca.[37] Following other events, the various participants enter one of the kivas. Shortly thereafter, a puppeteer operating an attached cord causes a wooden bird puppet to run back and forth on a pole projecting out of the kiva, while a concealed whistler performs chirps and warbles; this performance serves to announce the entrance of *Kolowisi* in the drama.[38] Then one of the performers secretly pours water from a sacred spring and seeds (the same as those in the goggle eyes and "hearts" of the Horned Water Serpent puppets) into the *Kolowisi* puppet so that they spurt from his mouth. The ejection of this fluid serves as an omen: if it flows evenly, things will go well for the Zunis; if it flows in a jerky manner, sickness will occur.[39] Then, while the ceremonial fathers cover the eyes of the initiates, one of the performers throws grasses from a sacred spring through the kiva doorway so that they seem to have come from the mouth of the serpent. Each ceremonial father collects some of the seeds and water in a bowl which he gives to the initiate along with some of the grasses. At home, the boy's family drinks some of this water and sprinkles the rest on their stacked corn; they lay the grasses next to this corn. They plant the seeds, regarded as having special power, in"sacred" areas in the fields.[40]

Shalako

The Western Puebloan puppets I have discussed to this point constitute a category that falls somewhere between masks and motionless images or fetishes. Some might question the inclusion of this final example, the Zuni *Shalako* kachina, in the category of puppets; it could, perhaps, be more appropriately designated as a "body mask," yet it shares some significant features with the puppet-like images mentioned above. Although puppets are generally miniature representations of animals or personages, they can also be gigantic images.[41] The Zuni *Shalako* kachina is one such enlarged representation.

There are six *Shalako* kachinas, one from each of the six kivas that are, in turn, associated with the six directions. They are giant bird-like figures, standing about ten feet tall (Figure 5). Barbara Tedlock has described these deities as "the visual antithesis of the Mudheads. They are stately, complex and pure while the Mudheads are silly-looking,

Figure 5. Zuni *Shalako* kachina preceded by his alternate. Drawing by M. Wright Gill, 1900. (Courtesy Smithsonian Institution, National Anthropological Archives).

simple and impure."[42] The head of the *Shalako* rests on top of a long cottonwood pole; the impersonator, who is inside the figure, carries this pole in his hands, supporting one of its ends in his belt.[43] Only the feet and lower legs of the impersonator are visible beneath this construction. The *Shalako* is the only kachina figure for which such a "body mask" is used; the other kachinas are characterized by masks that fit over the impersonator's head and a costume that is worn on the body. The garments of the *Shalako* figure are white embroidered blankets stretched over hoops of flexible willow; the impersonator sees by looking out through a triangular shaped opening in these blankets; although this opening is visible to the spectators, the impersonator must not get his face so close to it from the other side that he is visible. At certain points during the *Shalako* ceremony the impersonator leaves the figure by sticking the pole into the dirt so that the figure is upright while the hoop skirt collapses around it. *Shalako* is then said to be "sitting down." *Shalako's* face is painted turquoise; at either side of this face extend two horns from which one red and one white eagle feather hang. A crest of eagle and macaw feathers sits atop his head. Yellow macaw feathers adorn the black bangs of the forehead and eagle feathers are tied to a cotton string that runs the full length of the long black wig hanging down the back. A collar of raven feathers encircles the kachina's neck; two fox skins (said to be *Shalako's* arms) hang below these feathers and a dance kilt stretches across his shoulders. *Shalako* has large "goggle" eyes and a long wooden snout painted turquoise. Unlike that of any of the other kachinas this snout consists of two horizontal pieces; the impersonator operates the snout by pulling hidden strings so that the wooden pieces open and shut with a loud clattering sound.[44] Two impersonators for each *Shalako* figure, termed elder and younger brother, alternate bearing the "mask" throughout the ceremony.[45]

At the start of the *Shalako* ceremony, which usually occurs in early December, the six *Shalako* kachinas, in a procession with other kachinas and kiva members, enter the village in the early evening and go to the six houses that have been made ready for them.[46] Like the puppets discussed above, the *Shalako* kachinas also carry the seeds of plants vital to Zuni agriculture and ceremonialism; each kachina brings the seeds of wild plants, peaches, pumpkins, beans, and corn as "blessings" to the owner of the *Shalako* house where he will dance. After removing the "mask," the *Shalako* impersonators recite a long ritual prayer and then don the mask to spend the remainder of the night dancing in the house. The *Shalako* figure practically fills the front of the room and looks more than ever like a huge bird as it performs a back-and-forth running dance on tiny legs while emitting a high-pitched squeal and clapping its beak. The audience for this performance is made up of

Zunis, non-Zuni visitors, and the spirits of the Zuni dead who are believed to be present this night. Despite their stateliness, there is room for humor in the performance of the *Shalakos*. Sometimes they rush towards an audience member who has fallen asleep, clacking loudly while bending toward the individual. Startled, the dozer jerks awake and the audience laughs. The Zunis say that anyone who wants to sleep should have stayed at home, for this is a time when all of the spectators should be turning their minds to the central request of the ceremony—the prayer for rain in the coming year so that the crops may grow. At other times, the *Shalako* kachina will pursue one of the visiting Mudheads who has been teasing him, sometimes clapping his beak and chasing the little clown out of the window or a doorway, or even knocking him down and stepping on him. This is but one example of the humor which is frequently integral to major religious ceremonies of the Western Puebloans. The all-night performance ends at sunrise.

In the afternoon of that day the six *Shalakos* and their attendants assemble across the river from the main part of the village. A ritual race is conducted during which the *Shalakos* run, one at a time, to holes where they plant prayer sticks. The ground here is uneven, the "mask" ungainly, and the impersonators can barely see where they are going, but should the *Shalako* impersonator fall there will be bad luck for the village in the coming year. Spectators watch anxiously until the race is completed, gasping when the impersonator stumbles even slightly. Then the *Shalakos* leave the village, followed by a number of younger men who ritually hunt and kill the *Shalako*, a symbolic act that brings them success in hunting for the coming year.[47] The impersonators leave the "masks," and those who struck ("killed") the *Shalako* figures lay them out in state like deer that have been ritually killed.[48] Finally, the *Shalako* impersonators plant prayer sticks and return to the village; meanwhile, the *Shalako* attendants take the masks back to one of the ceremonial houses.

Analysis

Like other ritual dramas performed by the Western Puebloans, puppetry performances focus on a number of related goals, such as rain for the crops, success in the hunt, many children, and a long life. These, however, are often metaphors for the broader goals of increase and prosperity in general or for the satisfaction of a variety of specific needs relating to particular situations. The metaphoric, rather than directly literal, nature of such requests is underlined by the interesting adaptation of the Zunis to modern circumstances reported by Barbara Tedlock.[49] Traditionally, summer rain dancers have carried corn kernels and seeds of important crops in their belts as the "heart" of their request.[50] As the economy of Zuni has shifted from a reliance on farming to a heavy dependence on the sale of jewelry and pottery, many dancers now carry a lump of turquoise instead of the seeds in their belts. Although the song text is couched in terms of the traditional request for rain, it is clear that rain is used here as a metaphor for prosperity in general and the increased sales of jewelry in particular.

The dramatic action of these puppetry performances is frequently a graphic depiction of the desired outcome: in the Hopi *Palulukonti* ceremony at Walpi, although the serpents knock over fields of corn, they are propitiated in the end and suckled by the mother of the kachinas; at the Zuni initiation ceremony, *Kolowisi* spurts forth seeds, water from a sacred spring, and grasses which symbolize long life for the initiates; and the ritual killing of the Zuni *Shalako* represents successful hunting in the ensuing year. Indeed, this sort of graphic depiction of what ought to happen is characteristic of much of Hopi and Zuni artistic expression. For instance, at Zuni, both images painted on pottery and those carved on rocks frequently represent water beings who will bring rain to the fields, or deer figures that are emblematic of a successful hunt.[51] The various devices employed in the performances—screens depicting sun and cloud symbols, miniature fields of corn, conch shells, images of the Horned Water Serpent, bird figures, Corn Maidens, the recurrence of the number six (i.e., directionality), "hearts" composed of prayer feathers, corn kernels and seeds of important plants—are all part of the network of symbolic associations employed by the Hopis and Zunis to render their environment meaningful, a means by which they enact their particular vision of reality and the behavior appropriate to that vision.

Absence of improvisatory language is a feature of these puppet performances, as it is in Western Puebloan ritual drama in general. Although the Mudheads sometimes speak during their comic performances as part of the summer rain dances, their voices are muffled by their masks and they are often described as "talking backwards." Certain texts such as ritual prayers and kachina dance songs[52] are central to many performances, but neither the overt action nor the implicit meaning of the drama rely on a verbal exegesis. Nevertheless, there is a"text" which underlies all of Western Puebloan ritual drama. That text is the origin myth, the events of which are acted out in these dramatic performances. Central to these enactments are puppets which, in the context of the performance, no longer represent mythical beings, but *become* those beings and thus serve metonymically to evoke the entire text, merging the past with the present.[53] During the performance at Walpi, the blanket that the fire tender places in front of the fire as the stage is set creates shadows, a signal to the audience, perhaps, that what follows is illusory and requires the suspension of disbelief. Yet, in performance, the images become real, powerful, dangerous, and affective; similarly, in the ceremonies involving the kachinas, if the impersonator has a good heart, he becomes the god after donning the mask.

Ritual drama, a vehicle for the enactment of both appropriate and inappropriate behavior, serves both to reinforce and to challenge Western Puebloan world view. The comical Mudheads and the dignified kachinas might seem to be polar opposites in this respect, yet as discussed above, the Mudheads are both humorous and dangerous: they introduce chaos but, at the same time, they direct the performers of the rain dances; they call attention to the behavior of Zunis and others by mimicking that behavior, and they exert control over the villagers by carrying their footprints in the knobs that deform their heads. In the Walpi puppetry performances there is an ironic twist to the behavior of the Mudheads, for it is they who struggle with the serpents, attempting to control their disorderly conduct. Though certainly not an occasion for ribald laughter, there may be an element of humor implicit in such behavior. The Mudheads also appear as mediators in this performance; by acting as if the serpent puppets are real, they enhance their reality for the audience. Furthermore, Zunis and Hopis regard the Mudheads as having a special connection with the Horned Water Serpent;[54] each may be seen to embody the most dangerous aspects of Western Puebloan religion.

Even as the Mudheads enact both disorder and control, so too, is there a similar dual aspect to the behavior of the Horned Water Serpent. In Hopi and Zuni verbal art (i.e., myths and folktales), the Horned Water Serpent is most frequently characterized as dangerous—capable not only of bringing water, but bringing it in excess so that there are disastrous floods—but there is sometimes a comic side to the god as well. For example, in one Hopi folktale the Horned Water Serpent visits Coyote, coiling up in his house so that he fills the entire house and Coyote is pushed outside into the cold—an incident which is frequently greeted with laughter as the story is told.[55] Clearly the bringing of water is beneficial as well as harmful; thus the Horned Water Serpent is not only linked to procreation, but to its opposite—death—as well. In Zuni mythology, the Horned Water Serpent causes a flood which subsides only when the people agree to sacrifice a boy and a girl to the serpent. Yet the physical markers of this sacrifice, two stone pillars on the side of Corn Mountain that represent the girl and boy, are important fertility shrines, visited especially by parents who have been unable to have children.[56] One can compare this linkage of reproduction and death to the episode in the Zuni origin myth in which the witches bring corn to the people but demand in exchange the death of a child.[57] This dual aspect is apparent in the Walpi puppetry performance as well. The serpents knock over the fields of corn, yet they also have the power to bring the rain that is essential to the growth of corn and other vitally important foodstuffs.

Power is incorporated in the physical construction of the Horned Water Serpent puppets as well and is linked to a parallel symbolism in both the Mudheads and the kachina impersonators who perform during the summer rain dances. Not only do the round protuberances represent the serpents' eyes, they are also stuffed with seeds which, though invisible to the observers of the puppet performance, symbolize the central theme of all Western Puebloan ritual drama—fertility; the request for rain so that the crops will grow. Similarly, at both Zuni and Hopi, the "hearts" of the serpents, as well as the goggle eyes of the kachina masks and the "hearts" of the rain dancers, contain prayer feathers and seeds.[58] The "footprints" in the knobs on the heads of the mudheads and black butterfly wings in their drums are more directly related to power, but, again, symbolize an aspect of the performance that is "hidden" though nevertheless significant.

All three performances discussed above entail a certain amount of distortion of reality—the sort of incongruity that is frequently the basis for humor. For instance, at both Hopi and Zuni, the Horned Water Serpent sometimes behaves as if it were a human child, suckling a female kachina who is characterized as mother or great-great-grandmother of the gods. Yet this behavior follows what appears to be the wanton destruction of fields of corn. Similarly, the stately *Shalako* interrupts his dancing to "clack" at audience members who may have fallen asleep, to chase the impertinent Mudheads out the window, or to knock them down and step on them. Whether or not such behavior is the occasion for overt humor, it certainly serves to indicate that comedy and mystery are alternating aspects of the same event. But it is also clear that these two "moods" are not necessarily alternate in relationship to one another, but may actually be fused so that there is a dual meaning or value inherent in certain actions. Thus, the stumbling run of *Shalako* which may presage good or ill fortune or the attempt of a Mudhead to control one of the disorderly serpents by trying to ride it like a horse may be both funny and dangerous at the same time. In fact the special power, the affect, of such performances derives from this merging of contraries (humor and anti-humor, past and present) into one all-encompassing reality.

Acknowledgements

I thank my colleagues at the Pueblos of Hopi and Zuni for their commentary on this paper; I am particularly grateful to the families of Arlen Sheyka and Augustine Panteah for their hospitality and support during my various periods of fieldwork. I also thank Deborah Fant, Ted Frisbie, Joan Gross, Stephen McCluskey, Polly Schaafsma, and Ray Williamson for their comments and suggestions.

Notes

[1]By the term "Western Puebloan," I refer to the Hopi in Eastern Arizona and the Zuni in New Mexico. Some scholars also use this designation to include the Pueblos of Acoma and Laguna. The Zuni reservation contains only one village, the Pueblo of Zuni. The eleven contemporary Hopi villages are scattered over three mesas. For an excellent introduction to Hopi and Zuni prehistory, history, economy, social organization, and ceremonialism, see Alfonso Ortiz, ed., *Handbook of North American Indians*, vol. 9, *Southwest* (Washington, D.C.: Government Printing Office, 1979), pp. 467-586.

[2]Barbara Tedlock gives an overview of Zuni ritual drama and its relationship to Zuni world view in "Zuni Sacred Theater," *American Indian Quarterly*, 7:3 (1983), pp. 93-110.

[3]Sometimes, however, the Western Puebloans do place certain restrictions on audience attendance at ritual dramas. For instance, they do not allow pregnant women to attend the puppetry performances that involve the Horned Water Serpent, nor do they permit any women to touch any part of the puppets that represent this mythical being, perhaps because its association with fertility imbues it with power that is dangerous as well as beneficial. For a description of these restrictions see J. Walter Fewkes, "A Theatrical Performance at Walpi," *Proceedings of the Washington Academy of Sciences*, II (1900), p. 627n.

[4]Visual forms as metonymic of traditional narratives are discussed in Robert J. Smith, *The Art of the Festival* (Lawrence: University of Kansas Libraries, 1975), pp. 97-100, 140-141; and M. Jane Young, "Images of Power and the Power of Images: The Significance of Rock Art for Contemporary Zunis," *Journal of American Folklore*, 98:387 (1985), pp. 3-48. For a specific discussion of puppets as metonymic of the human drama, see Thomas A. Green and W.J. Pepicello, "Semiotic Interrelationships in the Puppet Play," *Semiotica*, 47:1/4 (1983), pp. 147-161.

[5]Mischa Titiev, "Old Oraibi, A Study of the Hopi Indians of Third Mesa," *Papers of the Peabody Museum of American Archaeology and Ethnology*, 22:1 (1944), p. 144. A somewhat similar dramatic enactment at the Hopi village of Walpi is described in Alexander M. Stephen, "Hopi Journal of Alexander M. Stephen," Elsie C. Parsons, ed., 2 vols., *Columbia University Contributions to Anthropology*, 23 (1936), p. 24.

[6]M. Jane Young, Tapes and Notes from Fieldwork (conducted with permission of Zuni Tribal Council) at Pueblo of Zuni, 1979-1981.

[7]This part of the Zuni origin myth is discussed in Ruth L. Bunzel, "Introduction to Zuni Ceremonialism," *Forty-seventh Annual Report of the Bureau of American Ethnology for the Years 1929-1930* (Washington, D.C.: Government Printing Office, 1932), p. 521; Frank H. Cushing, "The Zuñi Social, Mythic and Religious Systems," *Popular Science Monthly*, 21 (1882), pp. 4-5; J. Walter Fewkes, "A Few Summer Ceremonials at Zuñi Pueblo," *Journal of American Ethnology and Archaeology*, 1 (1891), pp. 22-24; Elsie C. Parsons, "Notes on Zuñi," Part 2, *Memoirs of the American Anthropological Association*, 4:4 (1917), pp. 229-237.

[8]Although they are Zuni clowns, the Mudheads occur in Hopi ritual drama as well, but one example of the extensive interchange between the two tribes.

[9]Ruth L. Bunzel, "Zuñi Katchinas: An Analytical Study," *Forty-seventh Annual Report of the Bureau of American Ethnology for the Years 1929-1930* (Washington, D.C.: Government Printing Office, 1932), p. 947; Elsie C. Parsons, *Pueblo Indian Religion* (Chicago: The University of Chicago Press, 1939), p. 105; Young, 1979-1981.

[10]For a description of the footprints contained in the knobs of the Mudheads see Elsie C. Parsons, "Notes on Zuñi," Part l, *Memoirs of the American Anthropological Association*, 4:3 (1917), p. 167; Elsie C. Parsons and Ralph L. Beals, "The Sacred Clowns of the Pueblo and Mayo-Yaqui Indians," *American Anthropologist*, 36:4 (1934), Table 1.

[11]The butterflies in the Mudheads' drums are discussed by Bunzel, "Zuñi Katchinas: An Analytical Study," p. 947; see also Parsons and Beals, ibid.

[12]This miming is discussed by Barbara Tedlock, "Songs of the Zuni Kachina Society: Composition, Rehearsal and Performance," in *Southwestern Indian Ritual Drama*, ed., Charlotte J. Frisbie (Albuquerque: University of New Mexico Press, 1980), p. 31.

[13]Young, 1979-1981; Elsie C. Parsons, "Winter and Summer Dance Series in Zuñi in 1918," *University of California Publications in American Archaeology and Ethnology*, 17:3 (1922), p. 193.

[14]M. Jane Young, "'Pity the Indians of Outer Space': Native American Views of the Space Program," *Western Folklore*, forthcoming. B. Tedlock, "Songs of the Zuni Kachina Society: Composition, Rehearsal, and Performance," pp. 22-23, refers to a song created for this event entitled "They Went to the Moon Mother." For a discussion of skits relating to the space program performed by another group of the Zuni clowns, the *Newekwe*, see Barbara Tedlock, "Boundaries of Belief," *Parabola* 4:1 (1979), pp. 70-72.

[15]Because these performances at Zuni and Hopi involving Horned Water Serpent puppets are considered sacred and closed to outsiders, I have never personally witnessed the events I describe here. I rely instead on descriptions in the ethnographic literature and some commentary I heard during my fieldwork at Zuni. I have been told, for instance, that the performances at both Hopi and Zuni are still part of the ongoing cycle of ritual enactments.

[16]The term "performing objects," is used by Frank Proschan in his overview, "The Semiotic Study of Puppets, Masks, and Performing Objects," *Semiotica*, 47:1/4 (1983), pp. 3-44.

[17]For a general discussion of the Horned Water Serpent in Hopi and Zuni religion, see Ruth Benedict, "Zuni Mythology," 2 vols., *Columbia University Contributions to Anthropology*, 21 (1935), p. 312; Bunzel, "Introduction to Zuñi Ceremonialism," pp. 515-516; Elsie C. Parsons, "A Pueblo Indian Journal, 1920-21," *Memoirs of the American Anthropological Association*, 32 (1925), pp. 56-57; Matilda C. Stevenson, "The Zuni Indians: Their Mythology, Esoteric Fraternities, and Ceremonies," *23rd Annual Report of the Bureau of American Ethnology for the Years 1901-1902* (Washington, D.C.: Government Printing Office, 1904), pp. 94-102.

[18]For a discussion of these six directions in relationship to Zuni ceremonialism, see Young, "Images of Power and the Power of Images: The Significance of Rock Art for Contemporary Zunis," pp. 16-18.

[19]The performance of the bird puppets at Zuni as part of the young boys' initiation is described in Stevenson, pp. 100-101. Fewkes, "A Theatrical Performance at Walpi," pp. 618-619, discusses the bird puppet enactments at Hopi as well as the performance of the corn grinding marionettes. Mischa Titiev, *The Hopi Indians of Old Oraibi: Change and Continuity* (Ann Arbor, The University of Michigan Press, 1972), pp. 324-325, describes a "puppet-doll dance" at the Hopi village of Hotevilla he witnessed in 1934 at which the bird puppets and corn maidens are central figures. Titiev identifies the bird as a sandpiper and the maidens as one Shalako and one Palhik maiden.

[20]For detailed descriptions (including drawings) of the construction of the Horned Water Serpent puppets used at Hopi and Zuni see Stephen, pp. 291-305; Stevenson, pp. 94-95 (as well as plates XIII and XIV); and Barton Wright, *Kachinas of the Zuni* (Flagstaff, Arizona: Northland Press, 1985), pp. 54-56. The comparison of the Horned Water Serpent puppets to a Chinese dragon is suggested by Hamilton A. Tyler, *Pueblo Gods and Myths* (Norman: University of Oklahoma Press, 1964), p. 245.

[21]I use the term "impersonators of the masked gods" after Bunzel "Zuñi Katchinas: An Analytical Study," pp. 902-903, but must note that the Zunis believe that when the impersonator dons the mask, he becomes the god.

[22]Though recorded descriptions by ethnographers focus on selected villages, several sources indicate that this dramatic performance is common to all the Hopi villages. See, for example, J. Walter Fewkes, "Hopi Katcinas Drawn by Native Artists," *Twenty-first Annual Report of the Bureau of American Ethnology for the Years 1899-1900* (Washington, D.C.: Government Printing Office, 1903), pp. 42-57; Stephen, pp. 287-333; Arlette Frigout, "Hopi Ceremonial Organization," in *Handbook of North American Indians*, vol. 9, *Southwest*, ed. Alfonso Ortiz (Washington, D.C.: Government Printing Office, 1979), p. 572, indicates that the *Palulukonti* ceremony continues to be performed by contemporary Hopis. It should also be mentioned that the *Palulukonti* ceremony described in this paper is not the only Hopi ceremony in which the Horned Water Serpent puppets occur, but it is the ceremony in which they take the most active part. For a discussion of the Horned Water Serpent effigy placed on the altar during other Hopi ceremonies (especially at the time of the winter solstice) see J. Walter Fewkes, "Tusayan Katcinas," *Fifteenth Annual Report of the Bureau of American Ethnology for the Years 1893-1894* (Washington, D.C.: Government Printing Office, 1897), pp. 270-271; Parsons, *Pueblo Indian Religion*, pp. 336, 503.

[23]Fewkes, ibid., states that if the Horned Water Serpent is not propitiated (during the Hopi winter solstice ceremony especially), it might hinder the journey of the sun along the horizon.

[24]See Stephen, pp. 287-349 for a fuller description of the construction of the puppets and the various screens, accompanied by excellent drawings. Fewkes, "A Theatrical Performance at Walpi," pp. 605-629, describes the performance with its various acts in some detail, including some excellent photographs.

[25]Ibid.

[26]Fewkes, ibid., p. 609. Although this particular performance occurred a number of years ago, ritual dramas at both Hopi and Zuni demonstrate considerable continuity over the past one hundred years.

[27]According to Fewkes, ibid., pp. 612, 618-619, 628, this part of the drama is sometimes performed by two masked girls instead of marionettes.

[28]Fewkes, ibid., p. 612.

[29]Fewkes, ibid., p. 615.

[30]See Fewkes, ibid., Plate XXXIV for a photograph of the serpents rising out of the jars (same as Figure 4 in this article).

[31]See especially Fewkes, ibid., p. 618 and Stephen, pp. 287-349.

[32]For further description of this act see Fewkes, ibid., p. 618; J. Walter Fewkes and Alexander M. Stephen, "The Palulukoñti: A Tusayan Ceremony," *Journal of American Folk-Lore*, 6:23 (1893), pp. 276-277. Stephen, p. 303 includes a drawing of the false arm.

[33]See Stevenson, p. 99 for a complete description of this puppet.

[34]For further explanation of these two initiations, see Bunzel, "Zuñi Katchinas: An Analytical Study," p. 975.

[35]For a description of the timing of this ceremony as occurring on "the day of the full moon of the third month following the [winter] solstice," see Bunzel, ibid., p. 976.

[36]Bunzel, ibid., p. 986.

[37]Stevenson, p. 99. Sometimes more than four blows may be delivered, especially if there is an indication that the boy has been "really bad." Ted Frisbie, personal communication, 1986.

[38]Parsons, *Pueblo Indian Religion*, p. 229n, mentions that one possible identification of the bird is "Sonora yellow warbler."

[39]Parsons, ibid., p. 448 discusses the ejection of fluid as an omen in this instance and others.

[40]See Bunzel, "Zuni Katchinas: An Analytical Study," pp. 975-980; Stevenson, pp. 94-102; and Wright, pp. 50-66 for more complete descriptions of the boys' first initiation procession and ceremony.

[41]"Giant puppets" are discussed in Jiří Veltruský, "Puppetry and Acting," *Semiotica*, 47:1/4 (1983), p. 92. It is of note that the Horned Water Serpent image discussed earlier is also a "larger than life" representation of a serpent.

[42]B. Tedlock, "Zuni Sacred Theater," p. 24.

[43]Parsons, *Pueblo Indian Religion*, p. 750n suggests that supporting the pole in this manner is due to European influence. She does not, however, include any data to support this suggestion.

[44]Parsons, ibid., also suggests European influence for this operation of the snout.

[45]For detailed descriptions of the *Shalako* figure and attendants and the ensuing "Coming of the Gods" ceremony, see Bunzel, "Zuñi Katchinas: An Analytical Study," pp. 941-975; Parsons, *Pueblo Indian Religion*, pp. 746-758; B. Tedlock, "Zuni Sacred Theater," pp. 100-108; and Wright, pp. 30-46.

[46]See Bunzel and B. Tedlock, ibid., for an explanation of the timing of Shalako ceremony and the building of the six Shalako houses.

[47]Parsons, "Notes on Zuñi," Part 1, p. 201.

[48]Parsons, *Pueblo Indian Religion*, p. 754n cites Bunzel's remark that this ritual is suggestive of killing of the god.

[49]Barbara Tedlock, "Kachina Dance Songs in Zuni Society: The Role of Esthetics in Social Integration" (unpublished Master's thesis, Department of Anthropology, Wesleyan University, 1973), pp. 69-70.

[50]Bunzel, "Zuñi Katchinas: An Analytical Study," pp. 873-874.

[51]See Young, "Images of Power and the Power of Images: The Significance of Rock Art for Contemporary Zunis," pp. 13-42. Although Hopi pottery is less

representational than Zuni pottery, other Hopi visual forms do center around such symbolic imagery.

[52]Zunis say the ritual prayers must be exactly the same, word for word, year after year; the kachina dance songs, however, are usually created anew for each dance set. See B. Tedlock, "Kachina Dance Songs in Zuni Society: The Role of Esthetics in Social Integration," pp. 90-92; Young, ibid., p. 26.

[53]Rock art images at the Pueblo of Zuni as metonymic of traditional narrative are described by Young, ibid., pp. 10-15. For a discussion of puppets as metonymic see Proschan, pp. 29-31 and Green and Pepicello, pp. 147-161.

[54]Parsons and Beals, pp. 496, 499, 507.

[55]For a recent rendition of this tale, see Ekkehart Malotki and Michael Lomatuway'ma, *Hopi Coyote Tales, Istutuwutsi* (Lincoln and London: University of Nebraska Press, 1984), pp. 9-21; mention of an older rendition occurs in H.R. Voth, "The Traditions of the Hopi," *Field Museum of Natural History Publication 96, Anthropological Series*, 8 (1905), pp. 184-188.

[56]For a discussion of these shrines, see Young, "Images of Power and the Power of Images: The Significance of Rock Art for Contemporary Zunis," pp. 29-30.

[57]The episode of the witches appearing and bringing corn is described in Ruth L. Bunzel, "Zuñi Origin Myths," *Forty-seventh Annual Report of the Bureau of Ethnology for the Years 1929-1930* (Washington, D.C.: Government Printing Office, 1932), pp. 592-593; Elsie C. Parsons, "The Origin Myth of Zuñi," *Journal of American Folk-Lore*, 36 (1923), pp. 137-138; Stevenson, pp. 29-31; Dennis Tedlock, trans., *Finding The Center: Narrative Poetry of the Zuni Indians*, by Andrew Peynetsa and Walter Sanchez (New York: Dial Press, 1972), pp. 258-263.

[58]Bunzel, "Zuñi Katchinas: An Analytical Study," pp. 873-874, 858; Stephen, p. 303.

Contributors

Fredrik E. deBoer teaches Theater at Wesleyan University. He is a specialist on Balinese drama and, in addition to many articles, is co-author (with I Madé Bandem) of *Kaja and Kelod: Balinese Dance in Transition.*

Kathy Foley teaches Theater at the University of California at Santa Cruz. She is a puppeteer who has carried out extensive research on Javanese puppetry.

Joan Gross has carried out considerable research dealing with the Belgian puppet tradition. This research has resulted in her Ph.D. dissertation and several articles on the subject.

Antonio Pasqualino is president of the Sicilian Association for the preservation of popular culture. He has written and directed puppet plays, adapting Sicilian folklore, history, and puppet traditions and is the author of a detailed study of Sicilian puppets, *L'opera dei pupi.*

Frank Proschan is a researcher at the Folklife Program of the Smithsonian Institution. He was an organizer of the 1980 International Conference on World Traditions of Puppetry and Performing Objects and is the editor of a special issue of *Semiotica* entitled *Puppets, Masks, and Performing Objects.*

Dina Sherzer teaches French literature and criticism at the University of Texas at Austin. Her research includes attention to linguistic and semiotic aspects of communicative forms. She is the author of *Modes of Representation in Contemporary French Literature.*

Joel Sherzer teaches Anthropology and Linguistics at the University of Texas at Austin. His research focuses on speech play and verbal art. He has written *Kuna Ways of Speaking: an ethnographic perspective.*

M. Jane Young teaches American Studies at the University of New Mexico. Her area of research is cultures and societies of the American Southwest, in particular the Zuni Indians. She has written several articles on material culture and folklore. Her first book, *Signs from the Ancestors: Zuni Cultural Symbolism and Perceptions of Rock Art*, a publication of the American Folklore Society, will be published in early spring 1988 by the University of New Nexico Press.